Contact me

Instagram

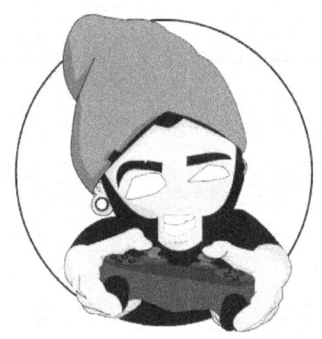

@bite2breakskin

follow me for more artwork or send me a direct message if you need to get in touch

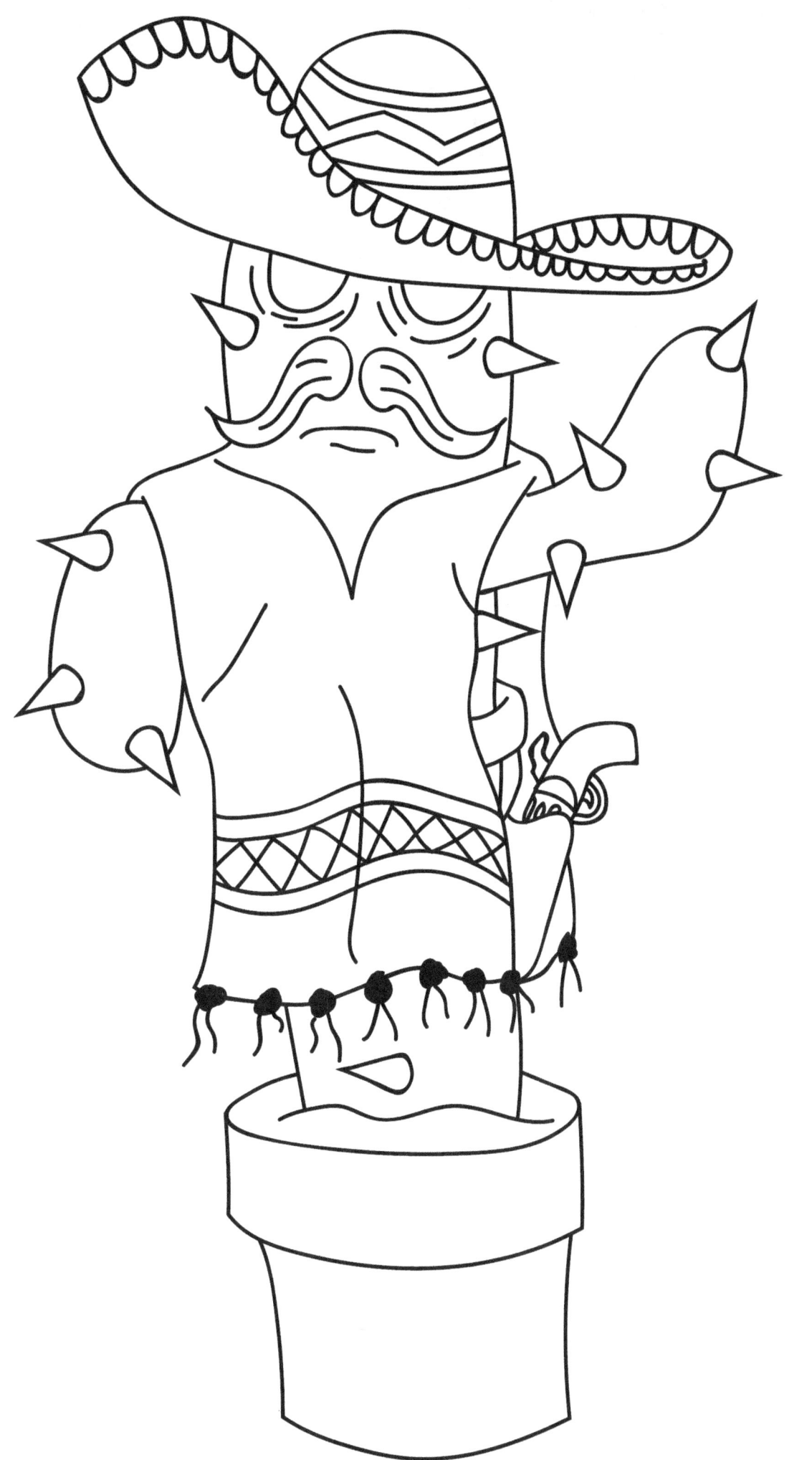

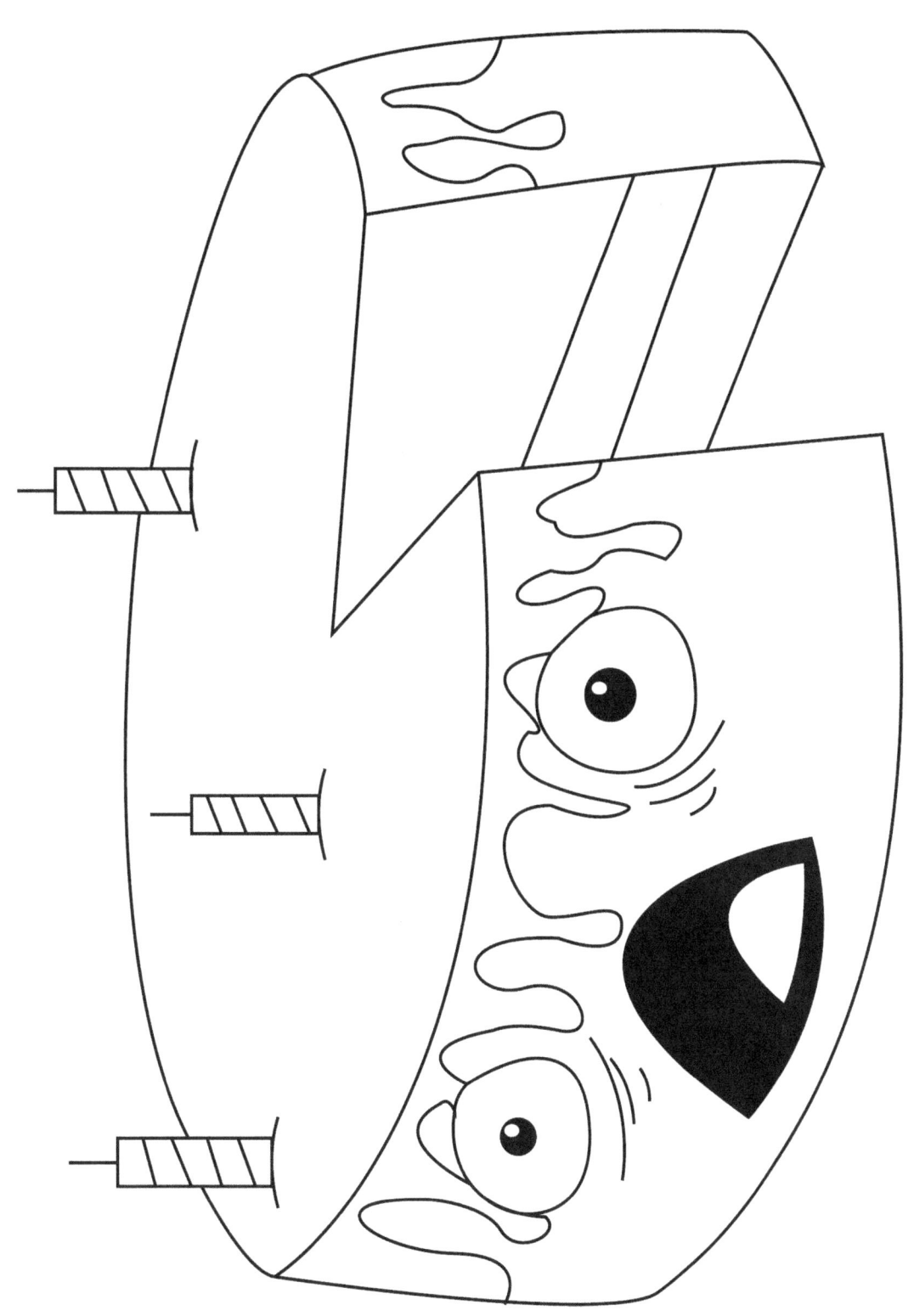

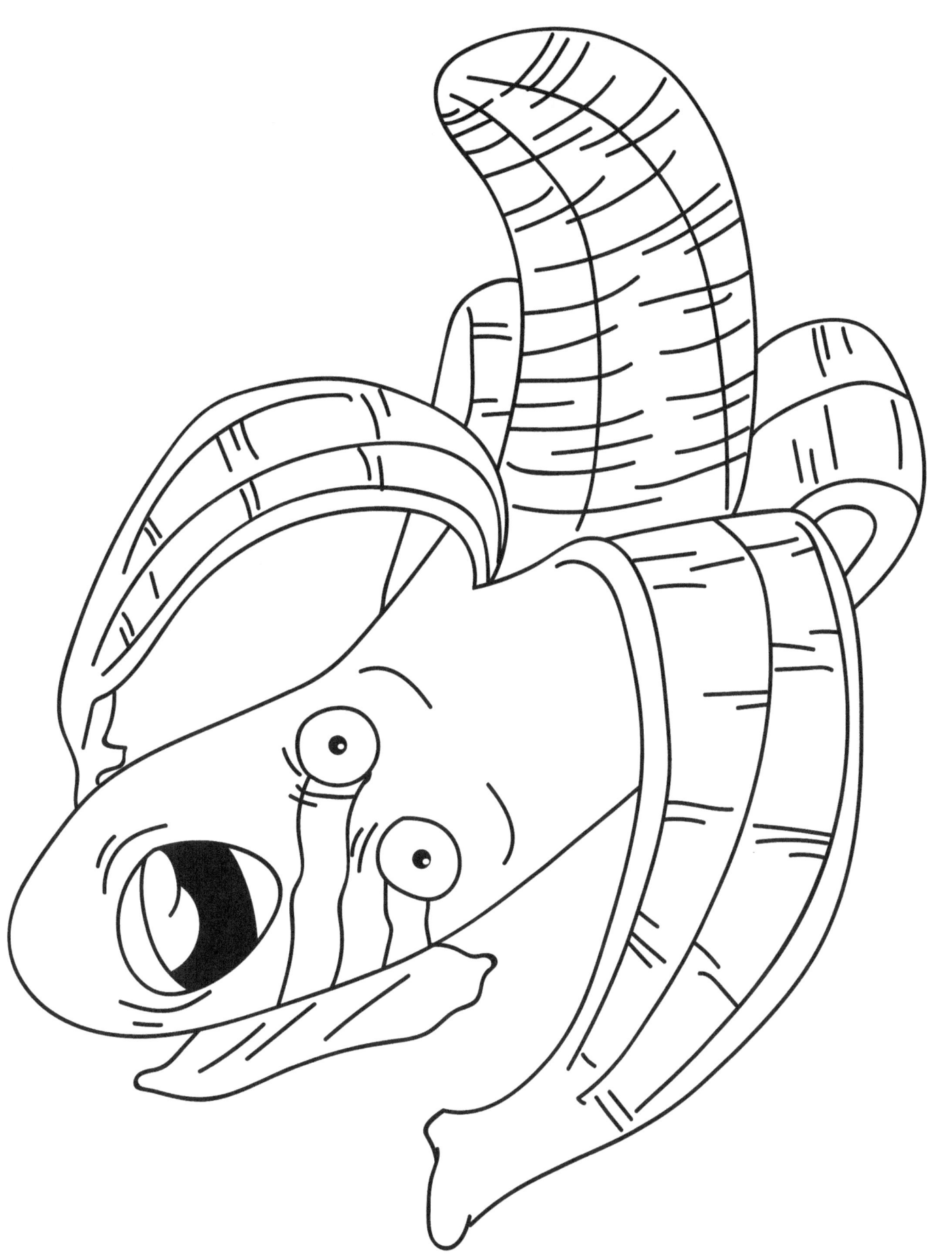

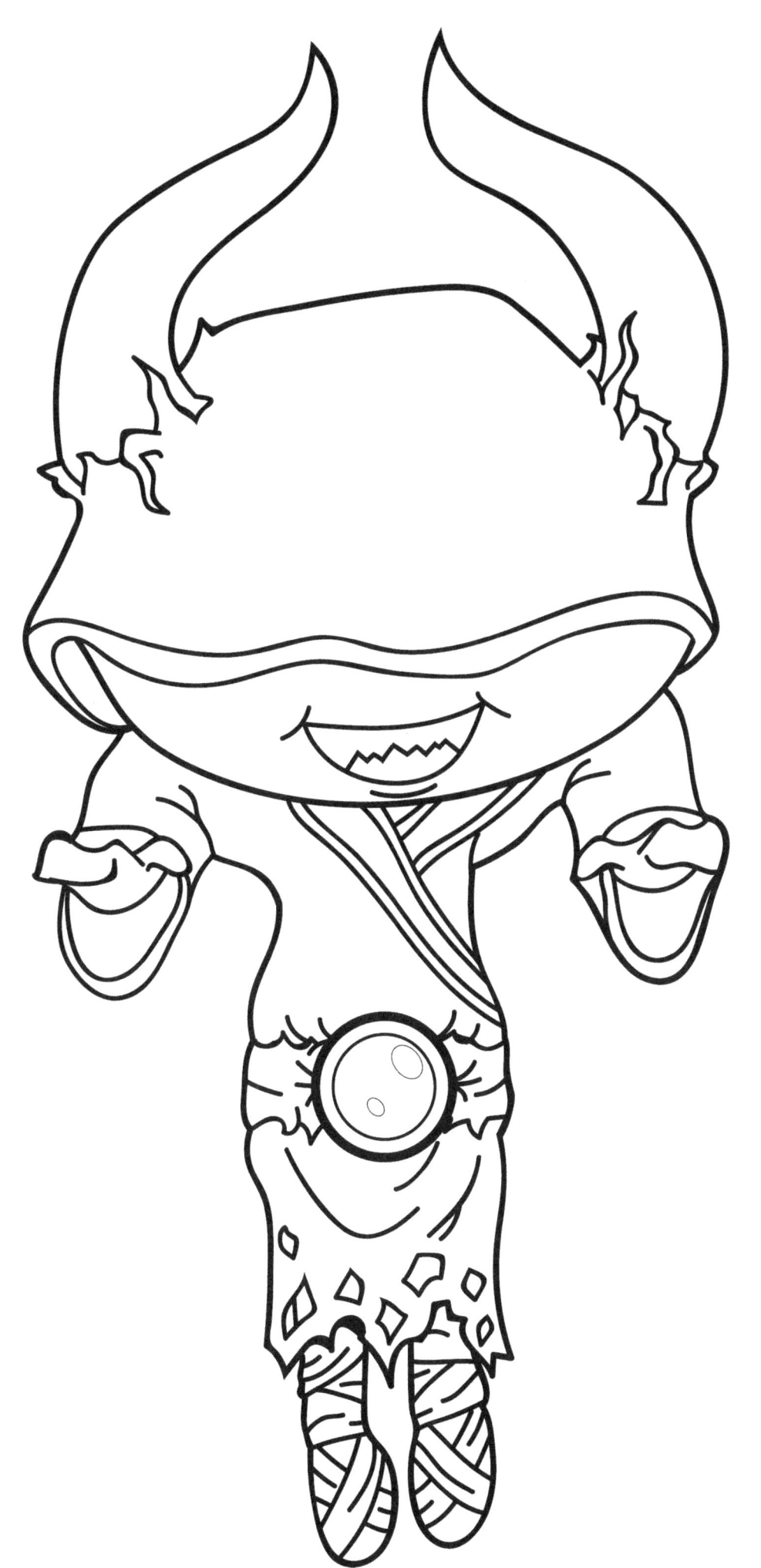

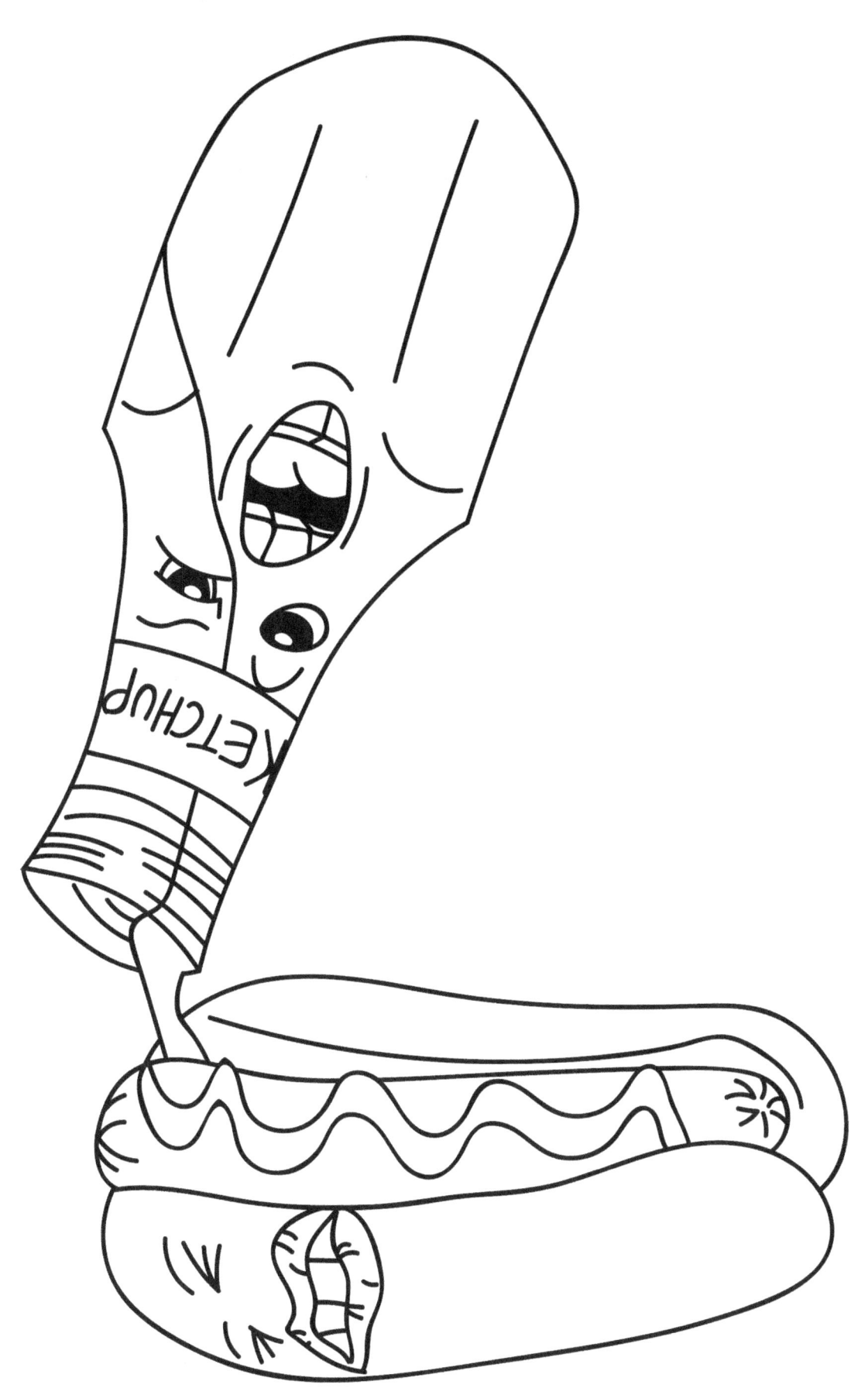

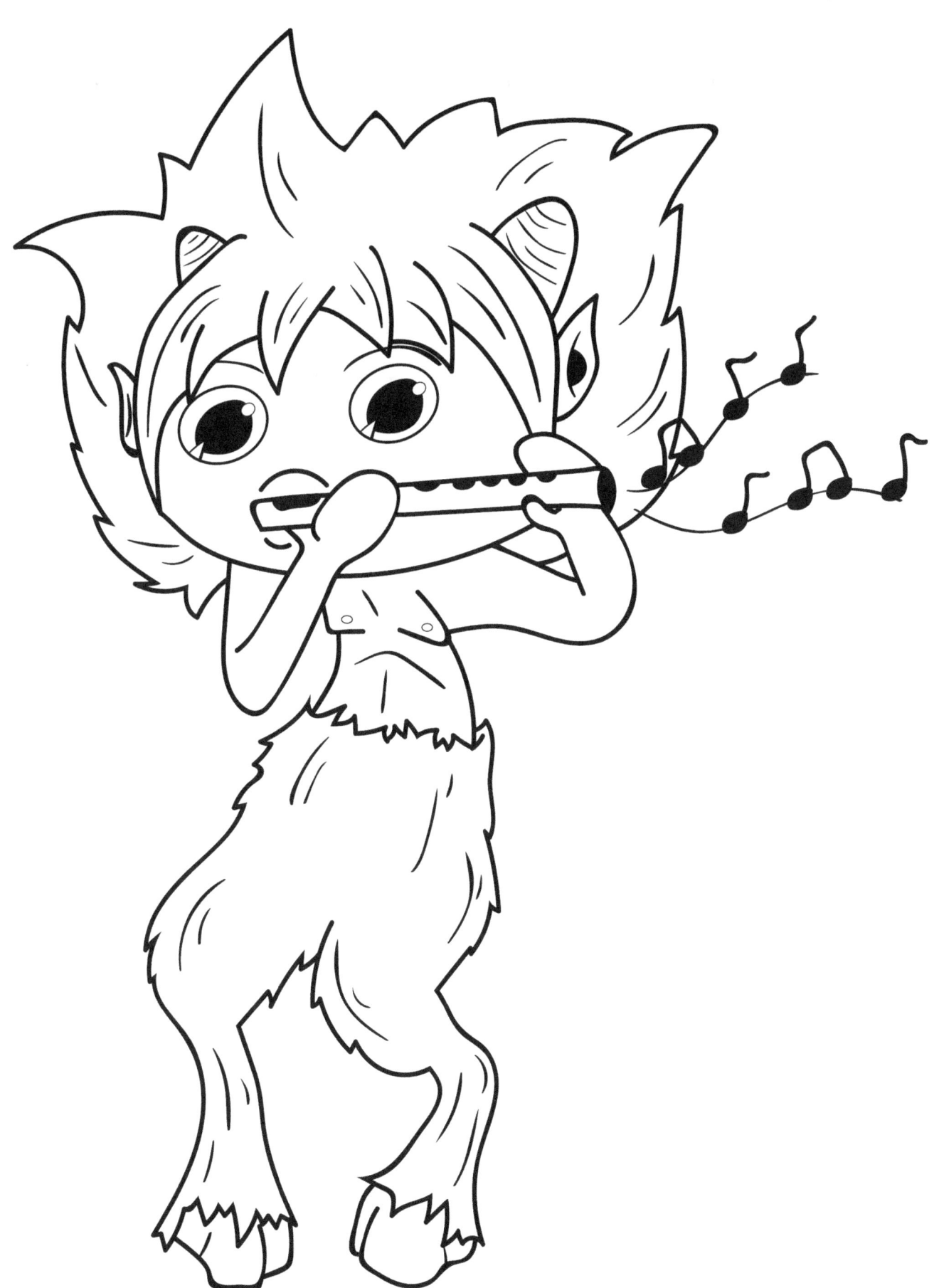

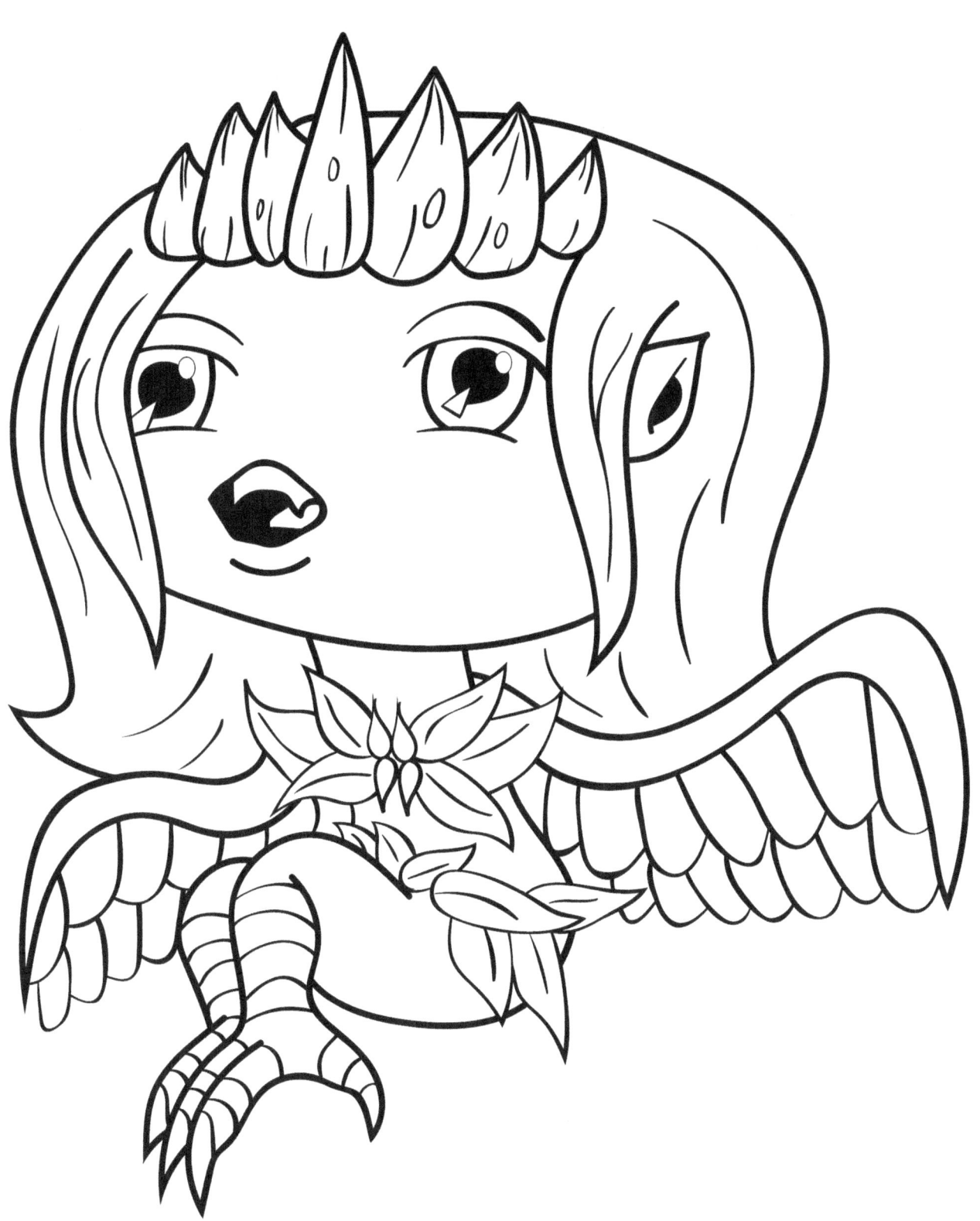

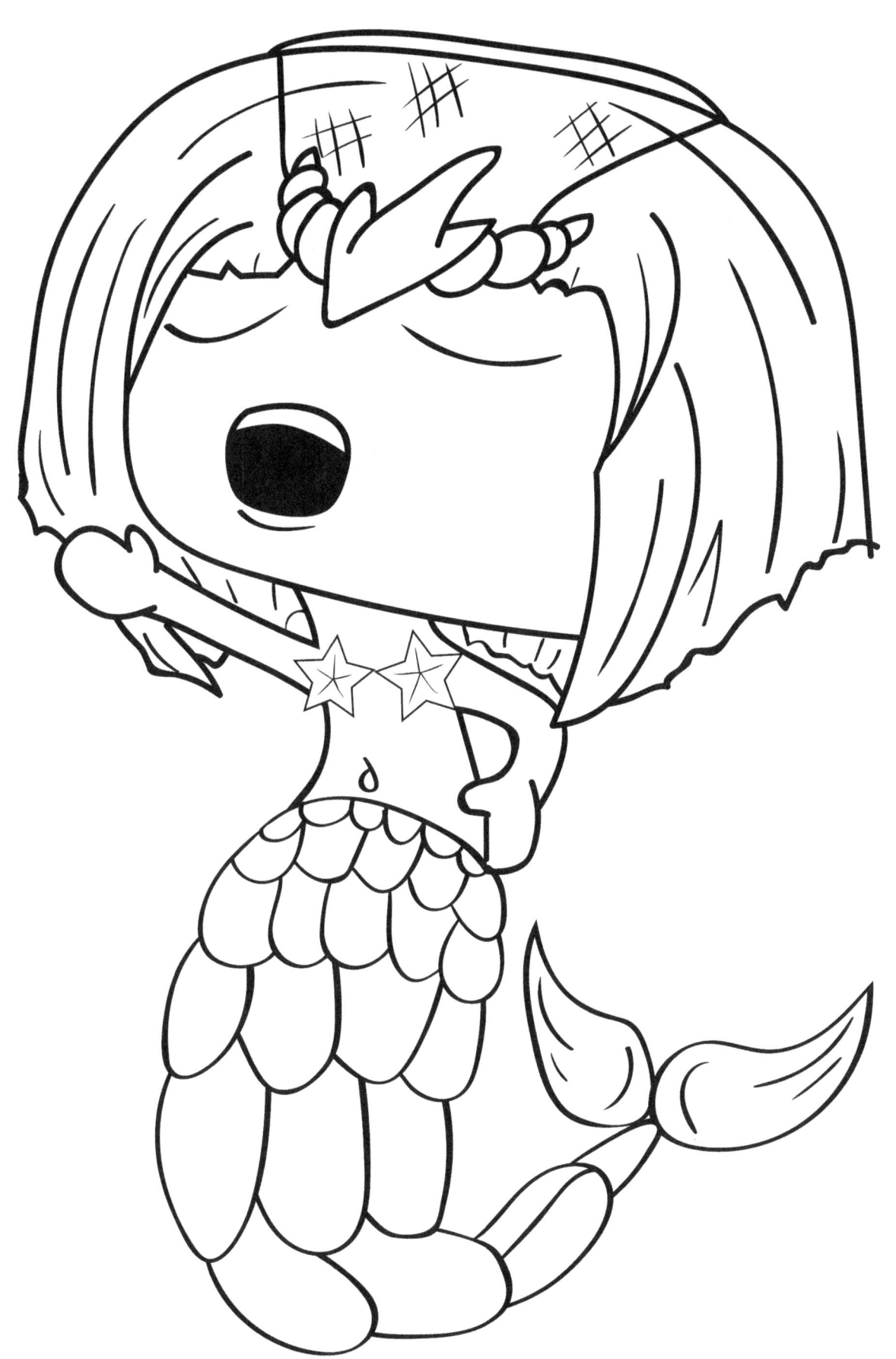

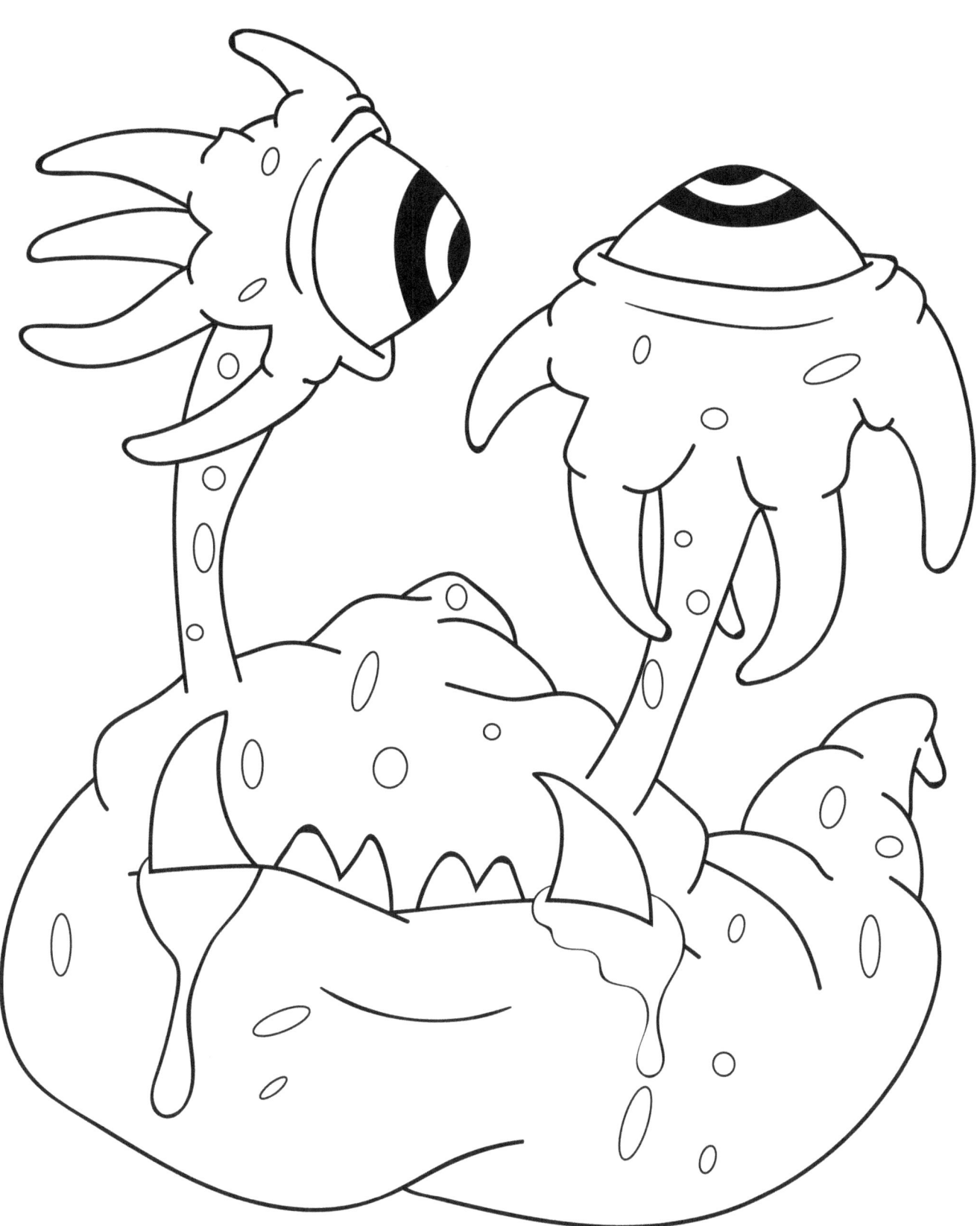

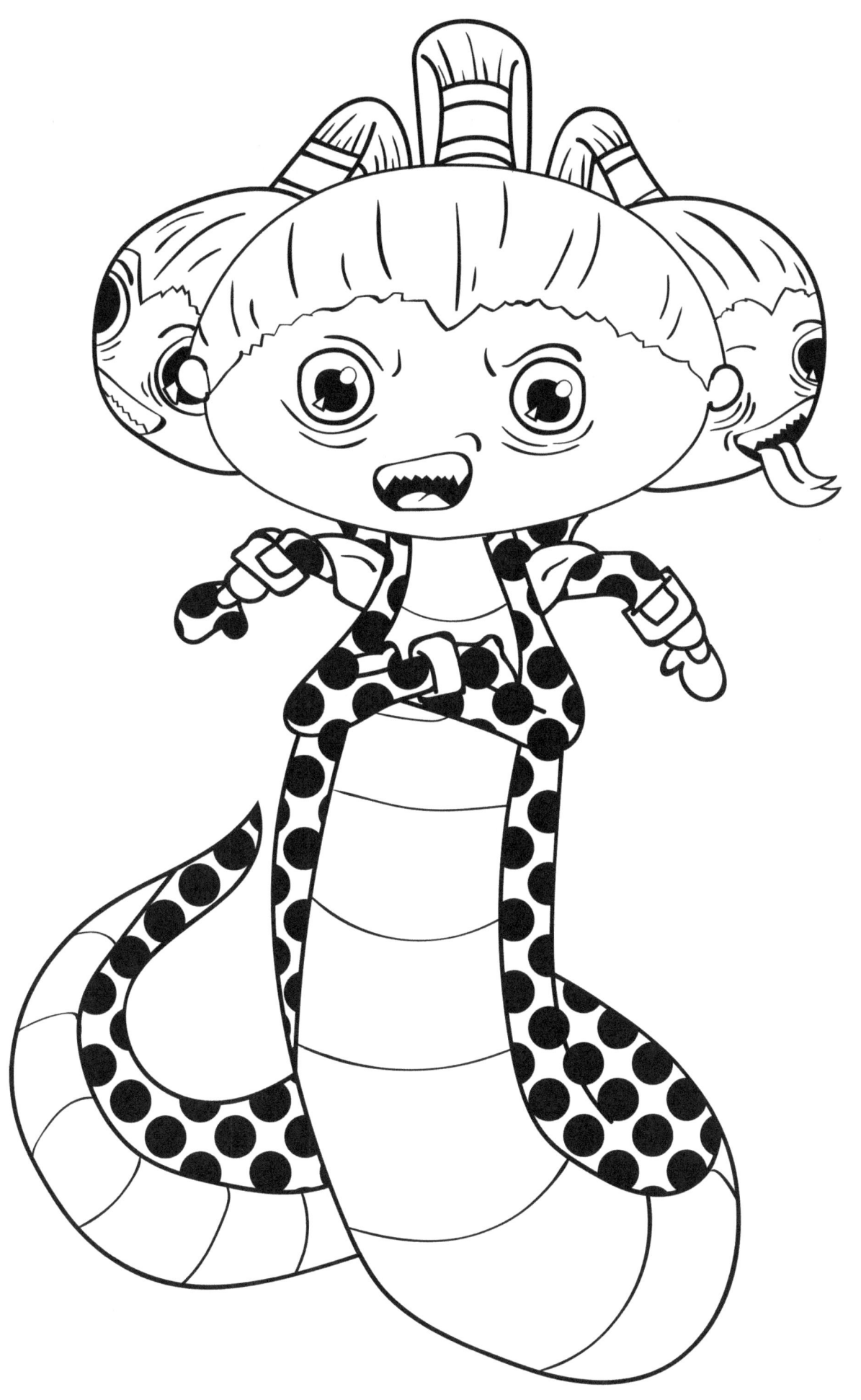

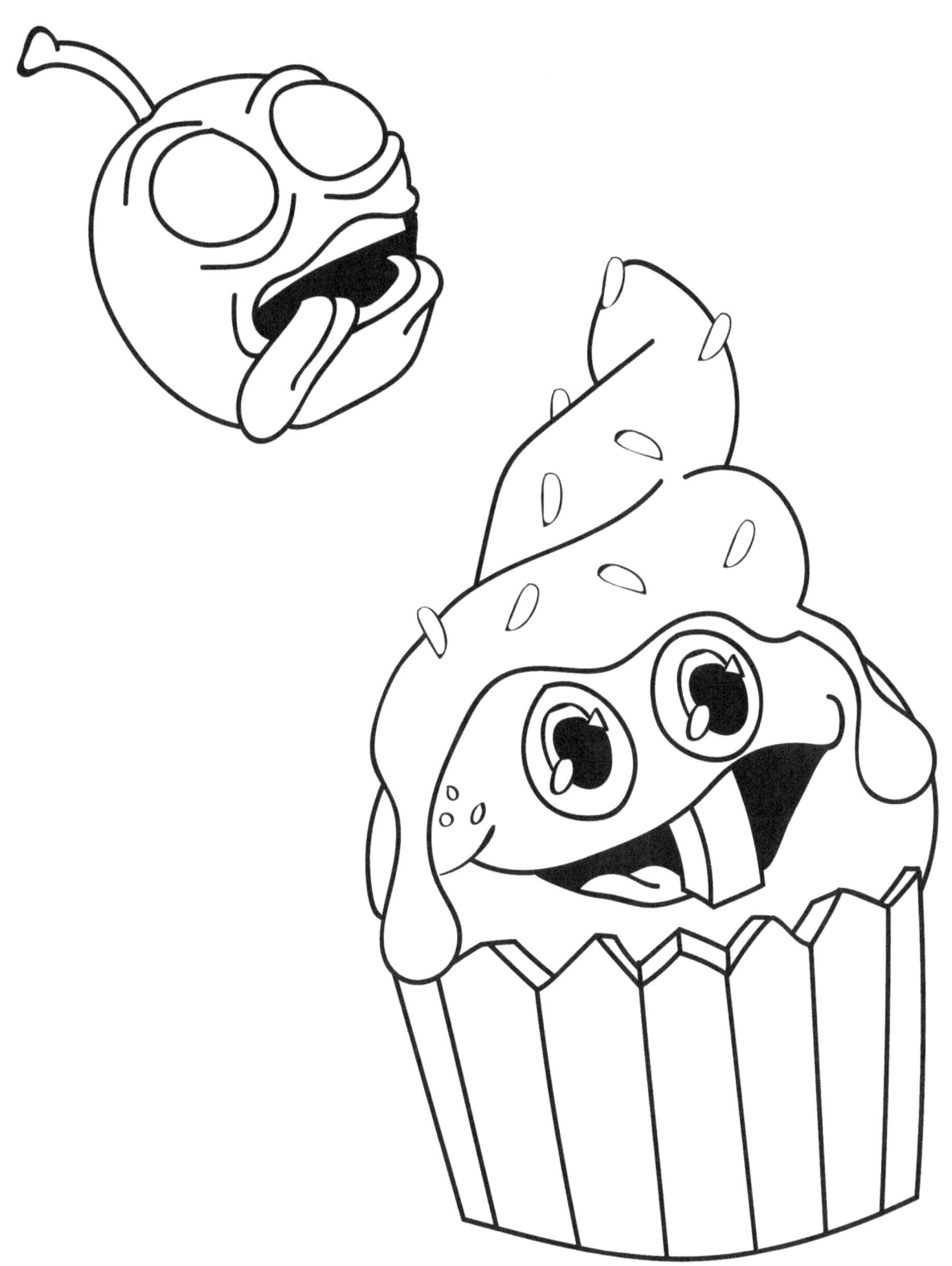

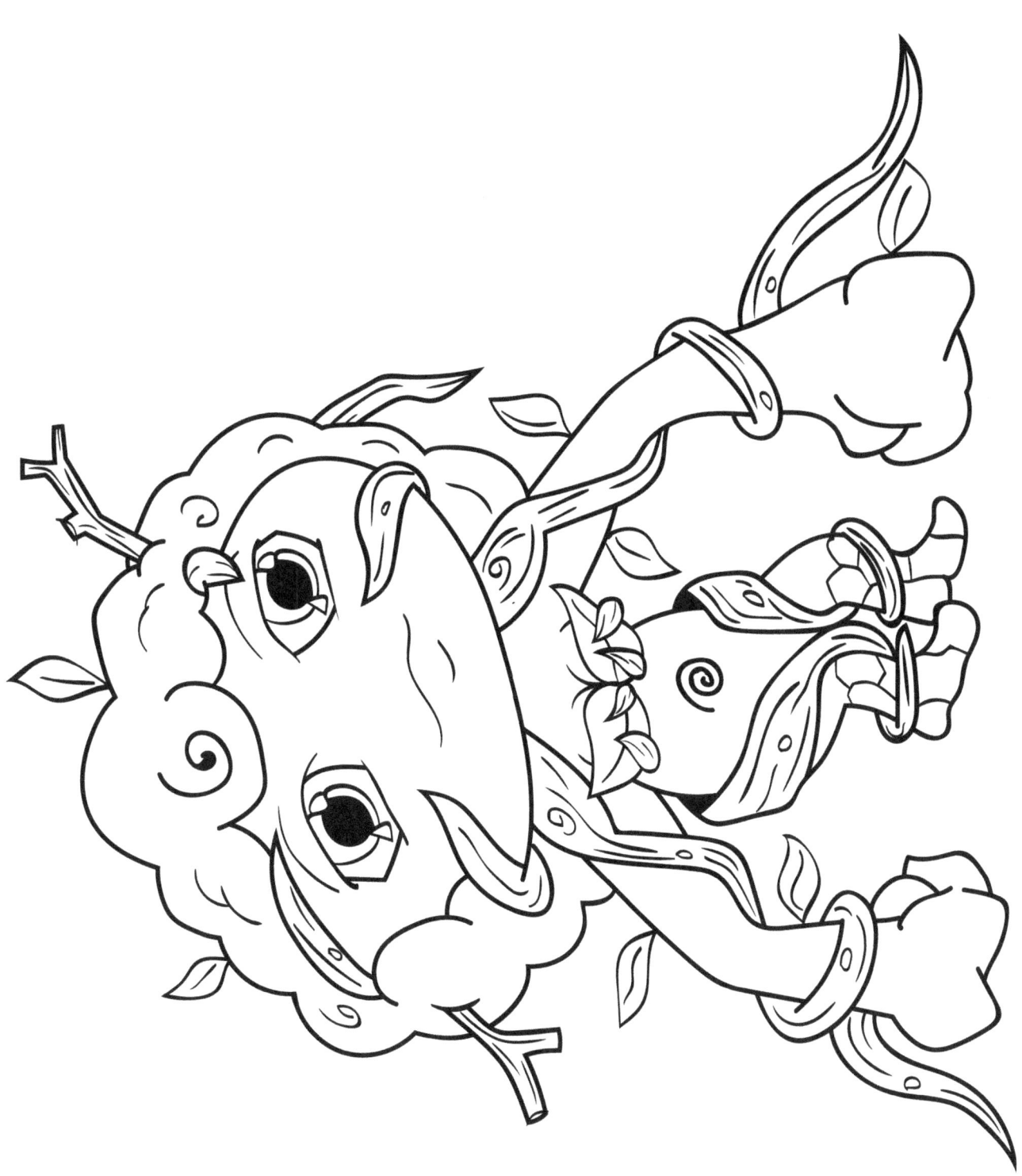

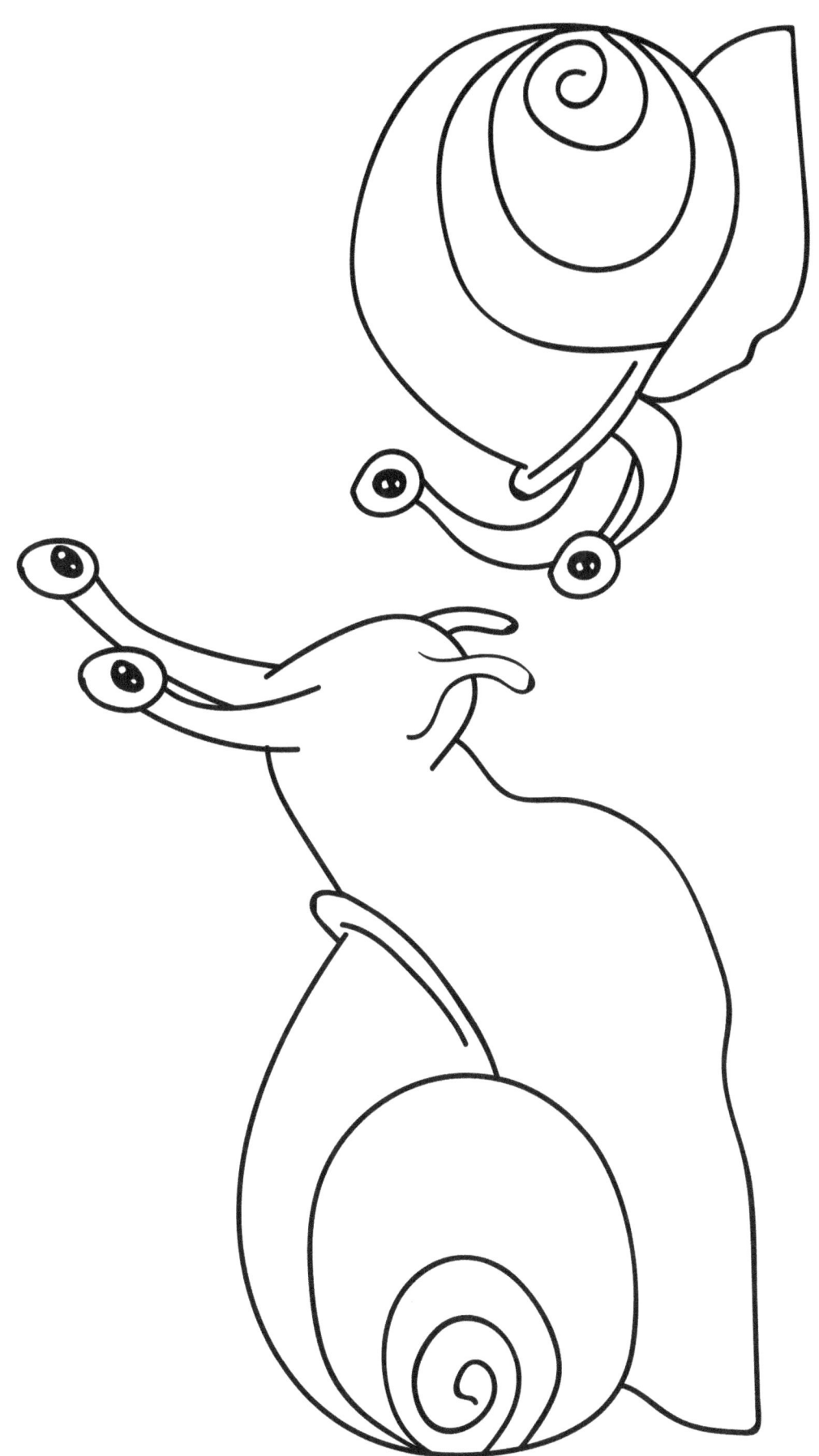

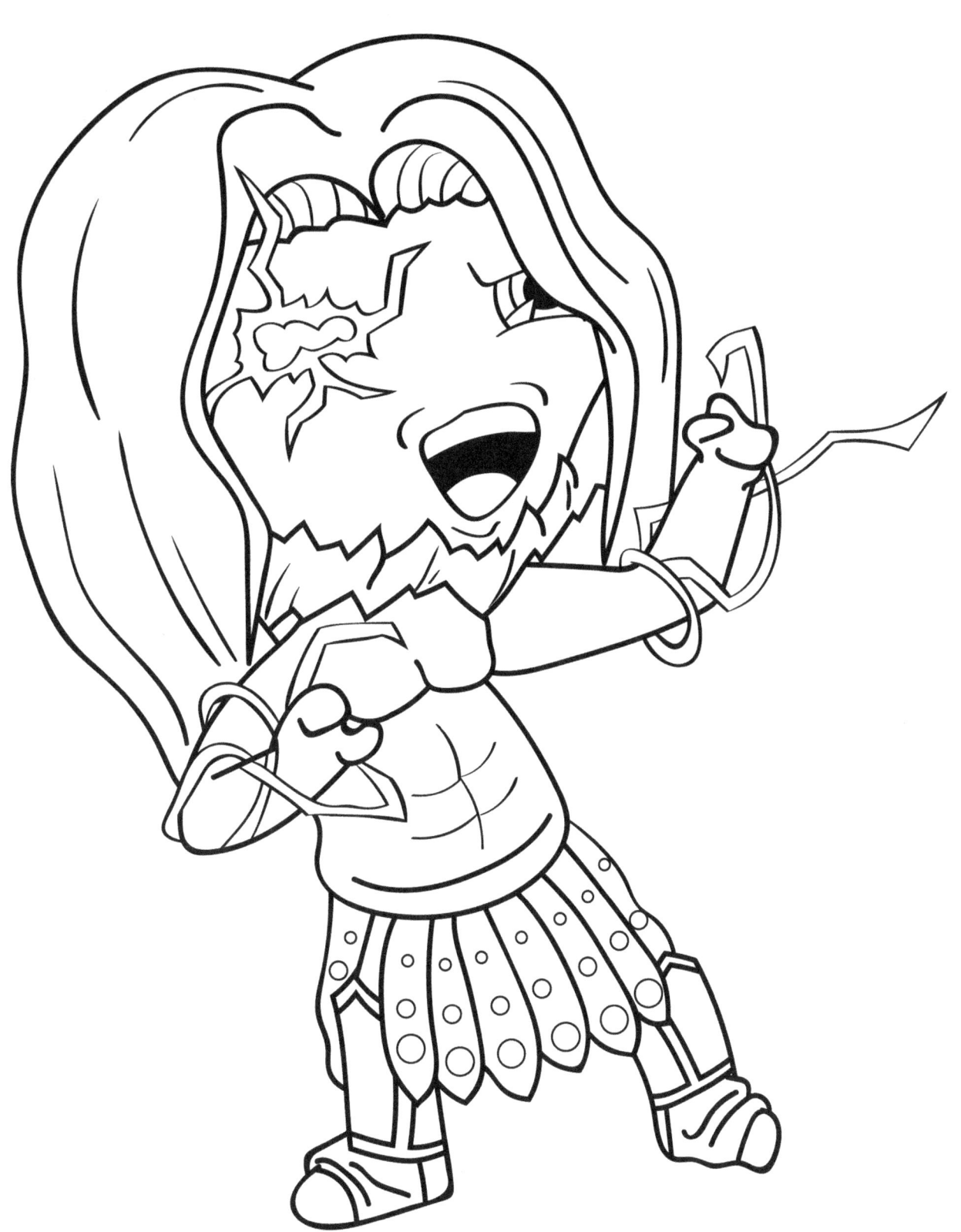

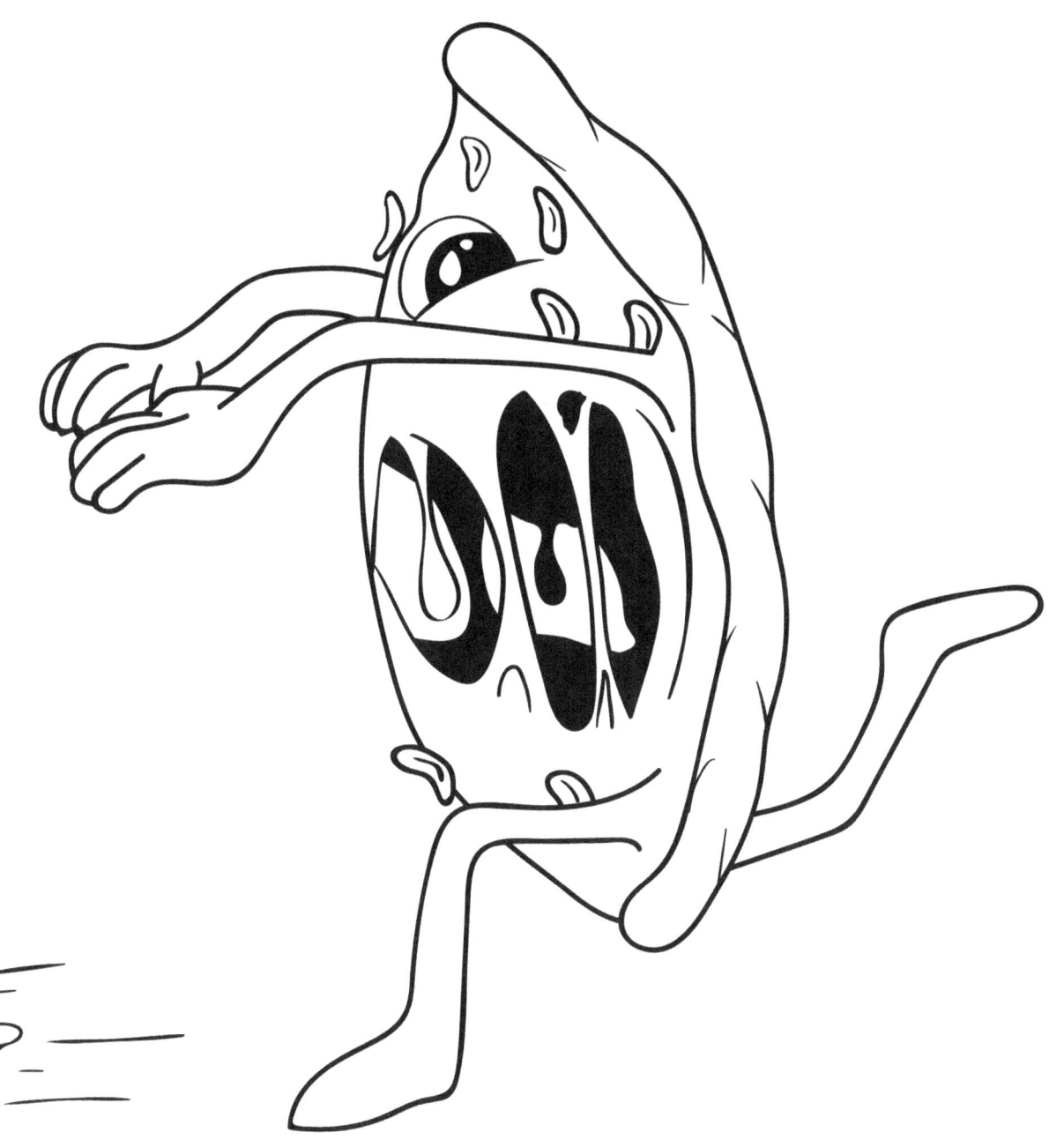

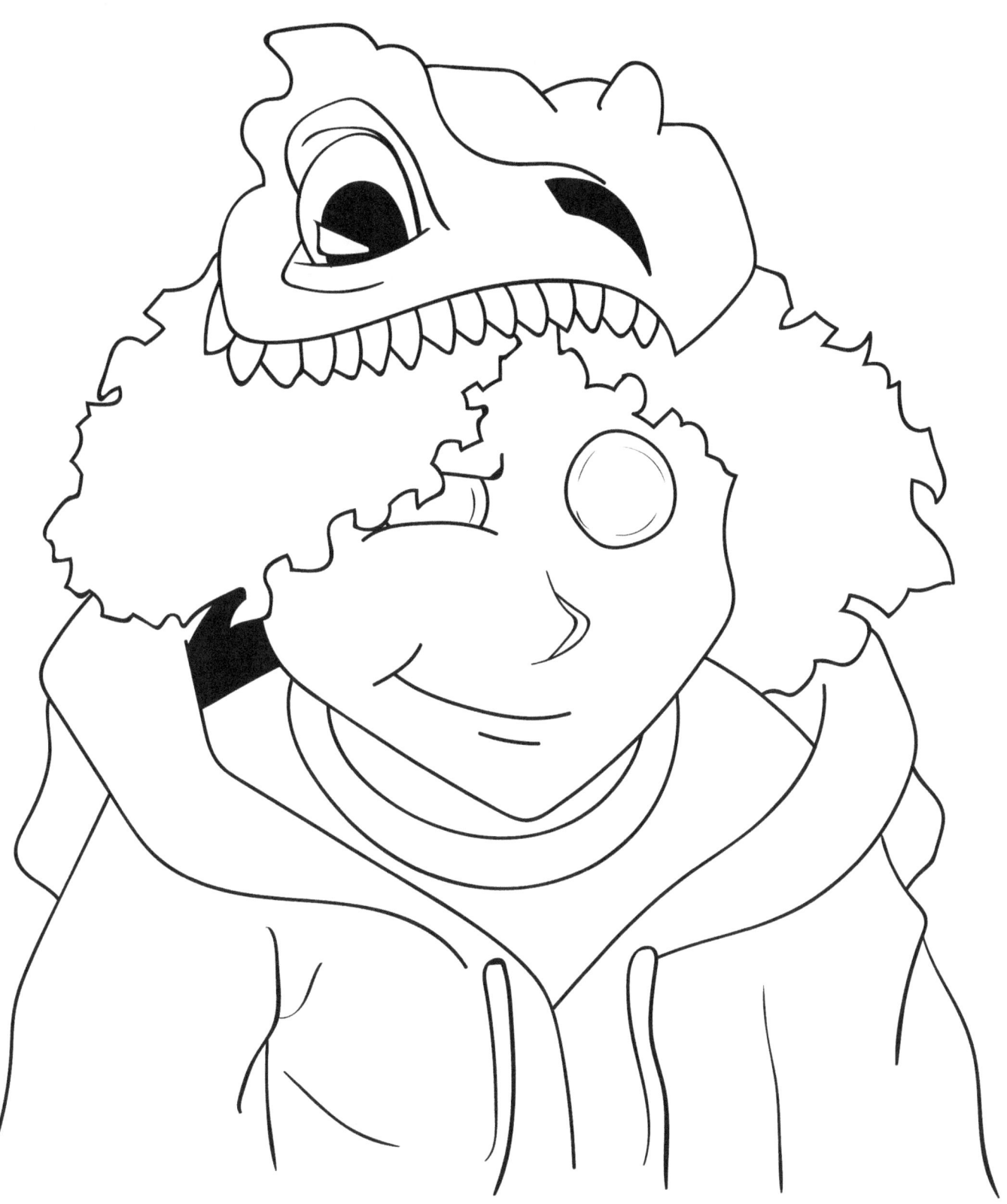

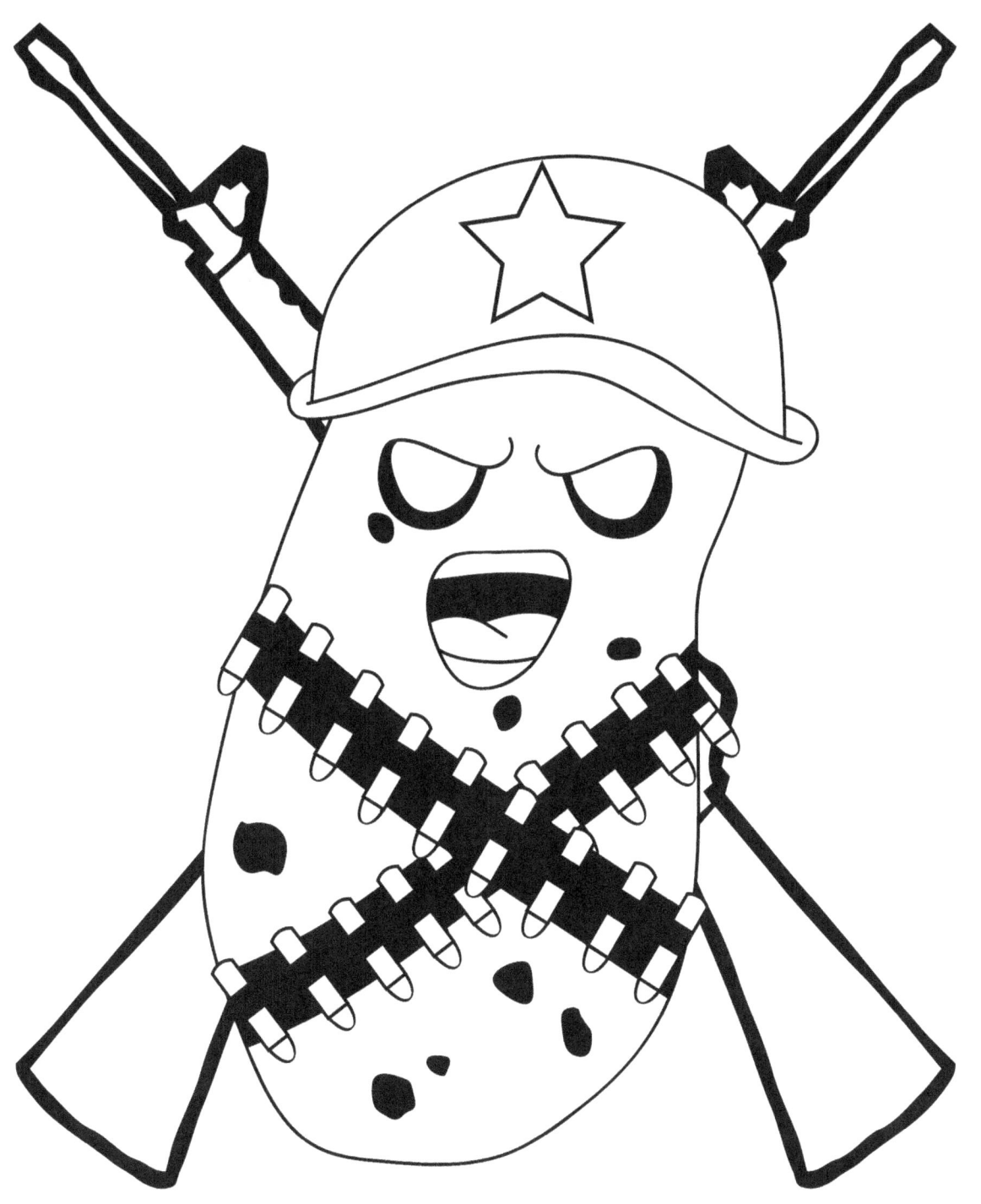

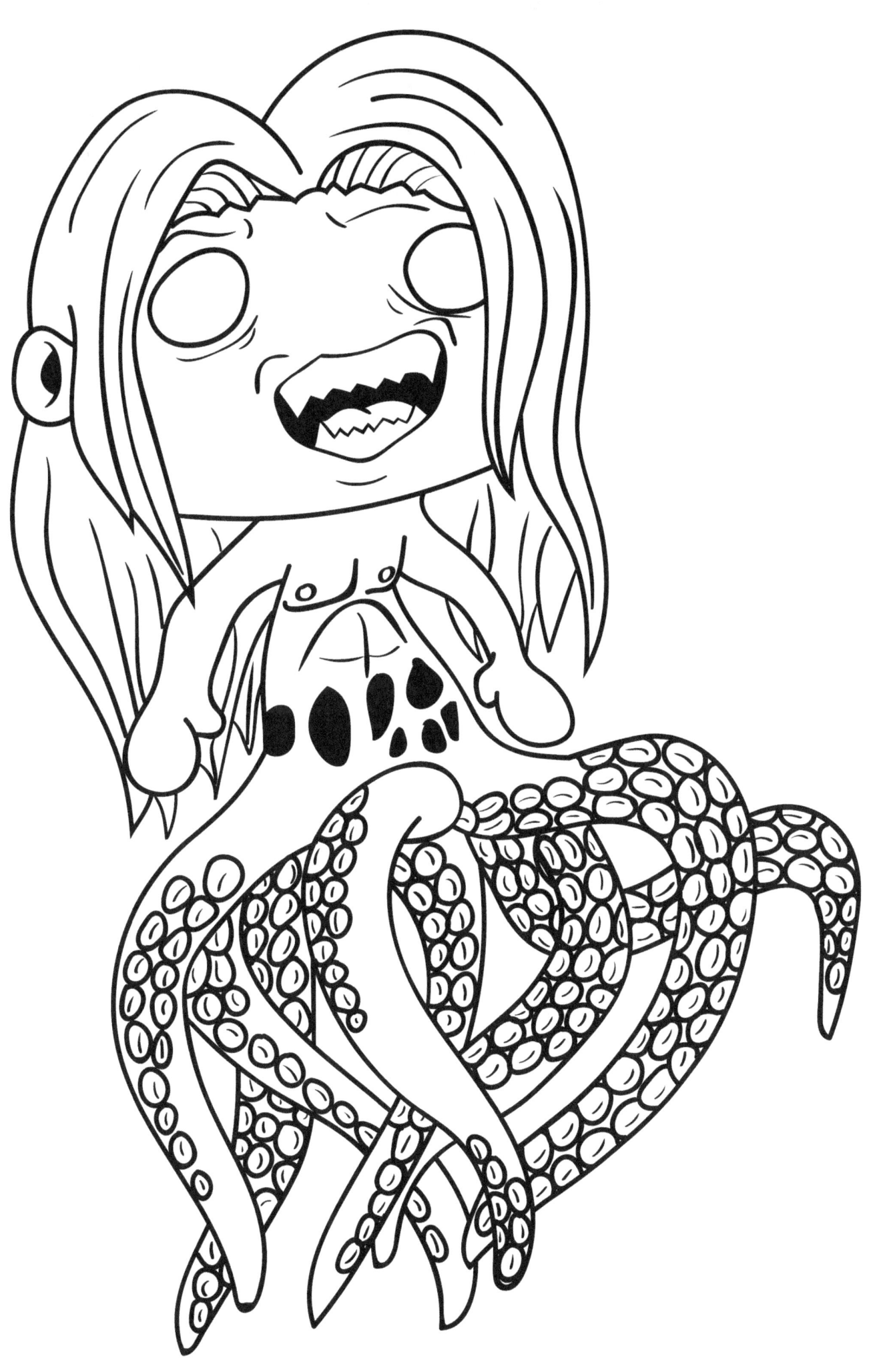

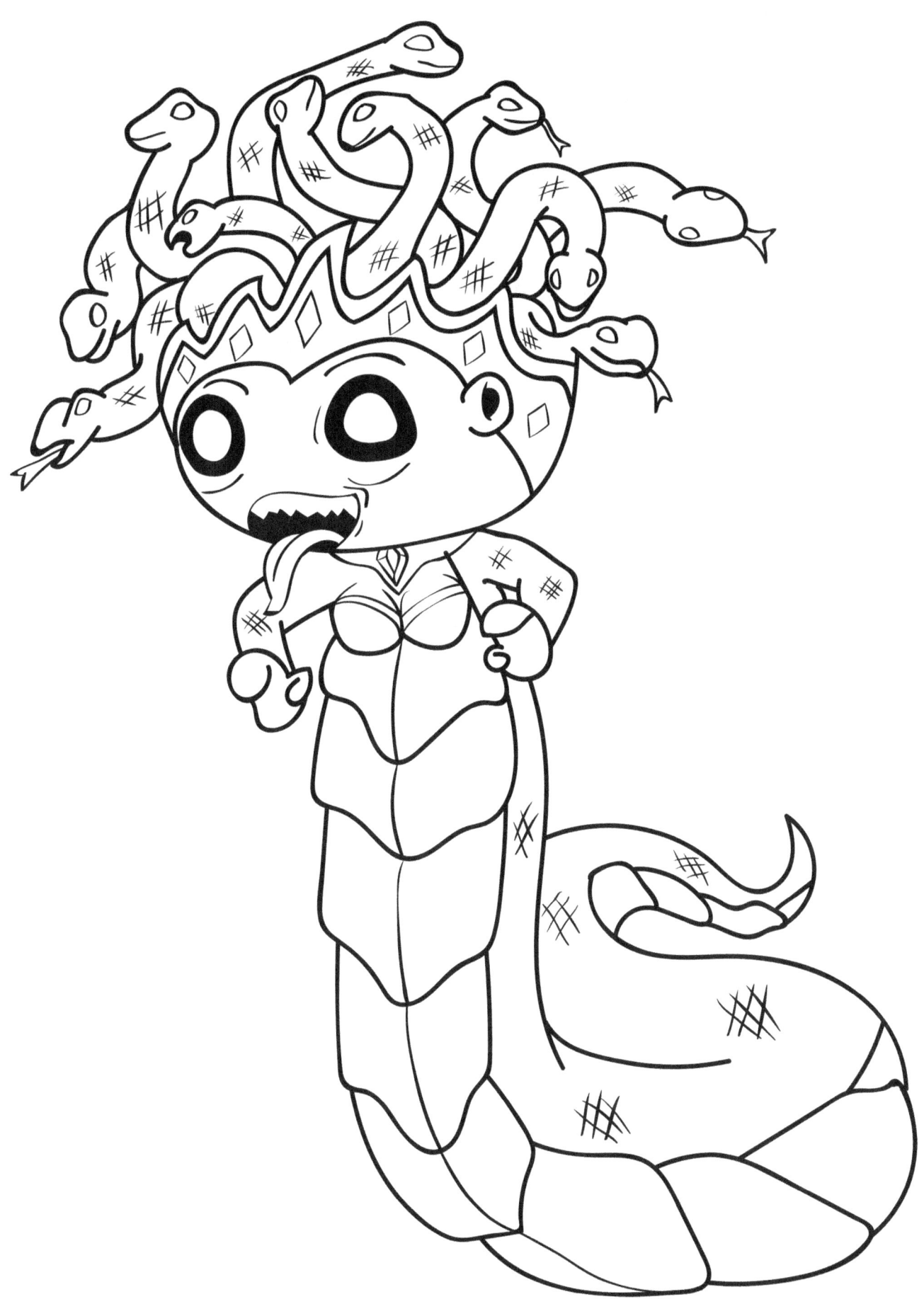

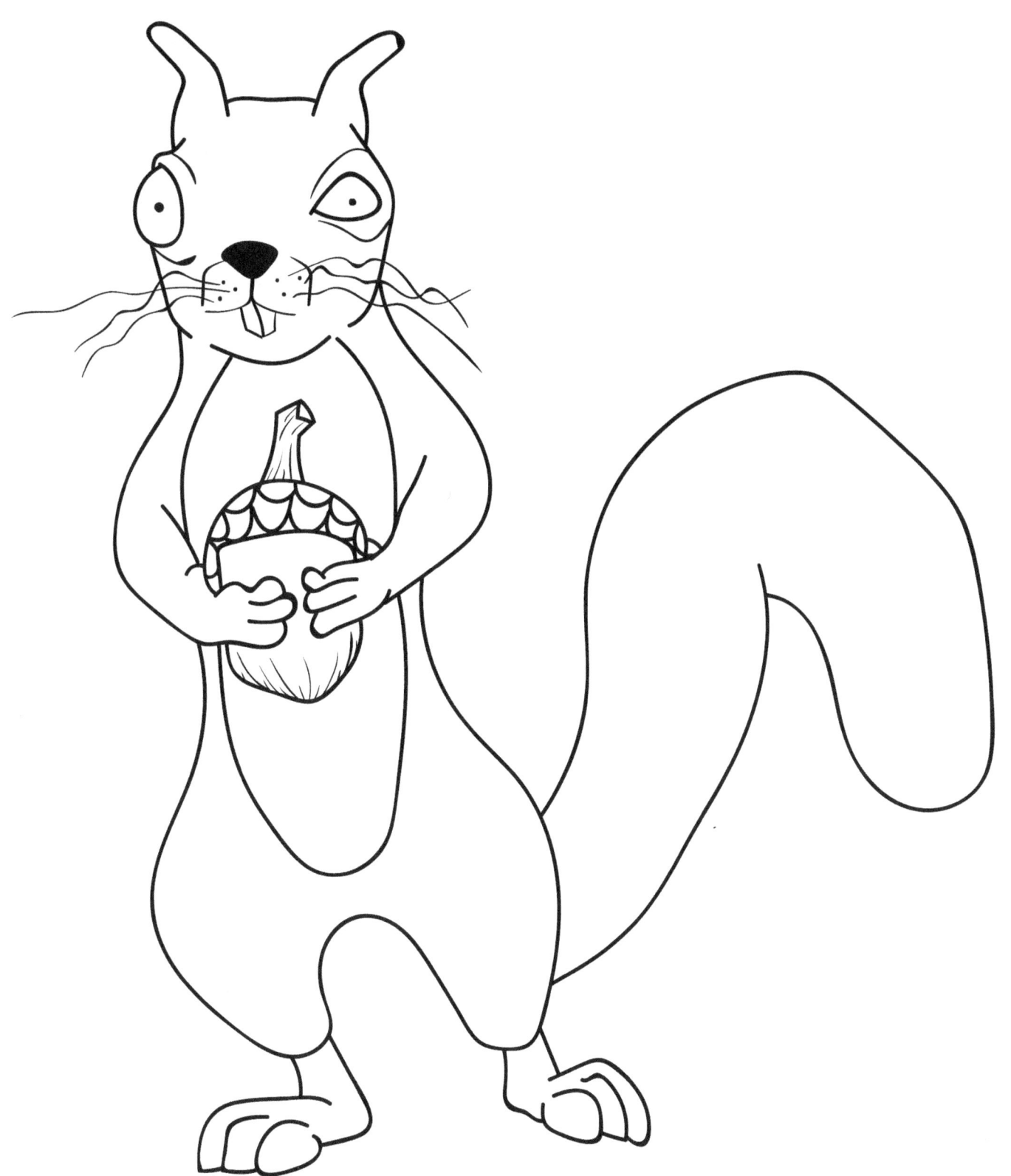

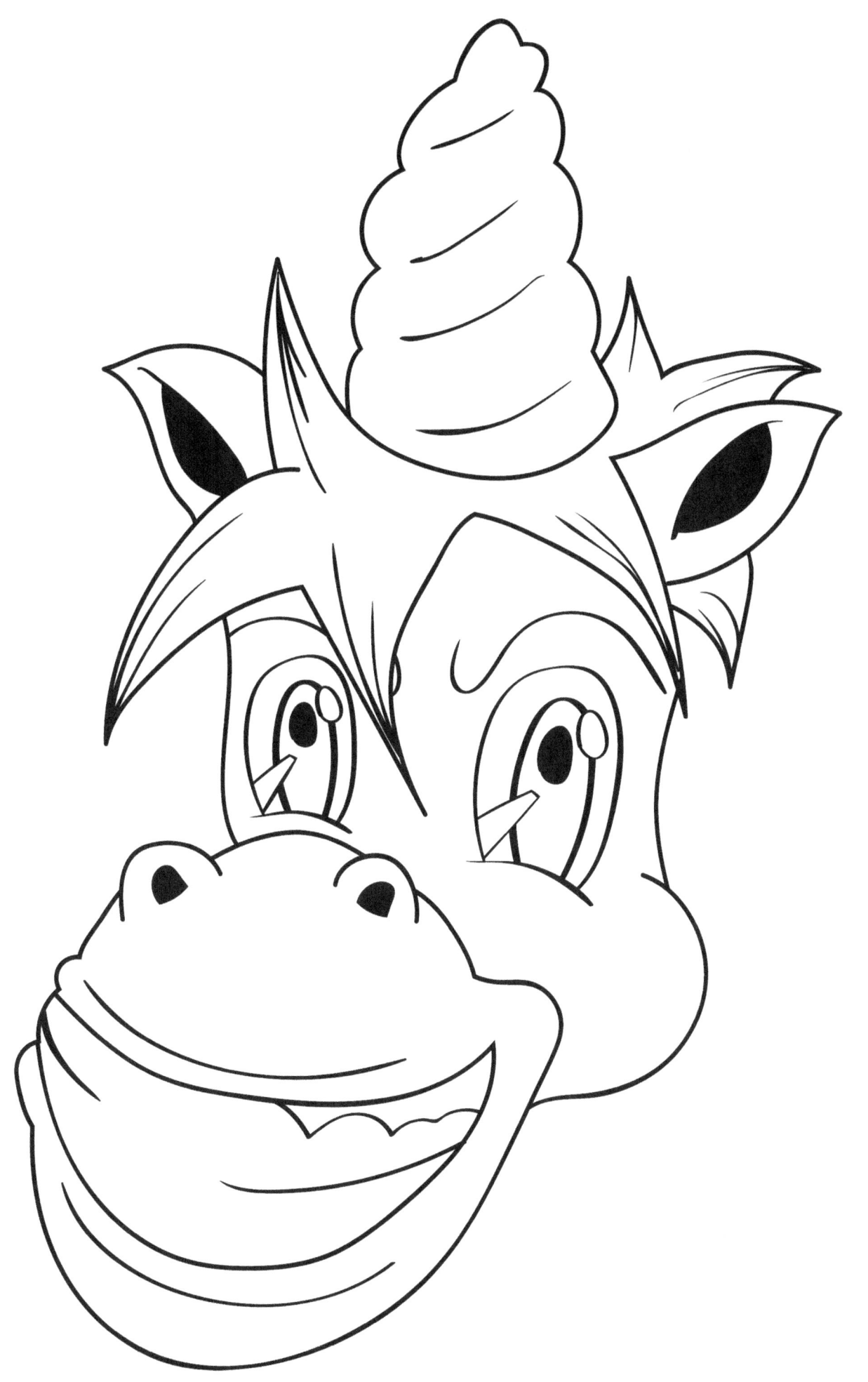

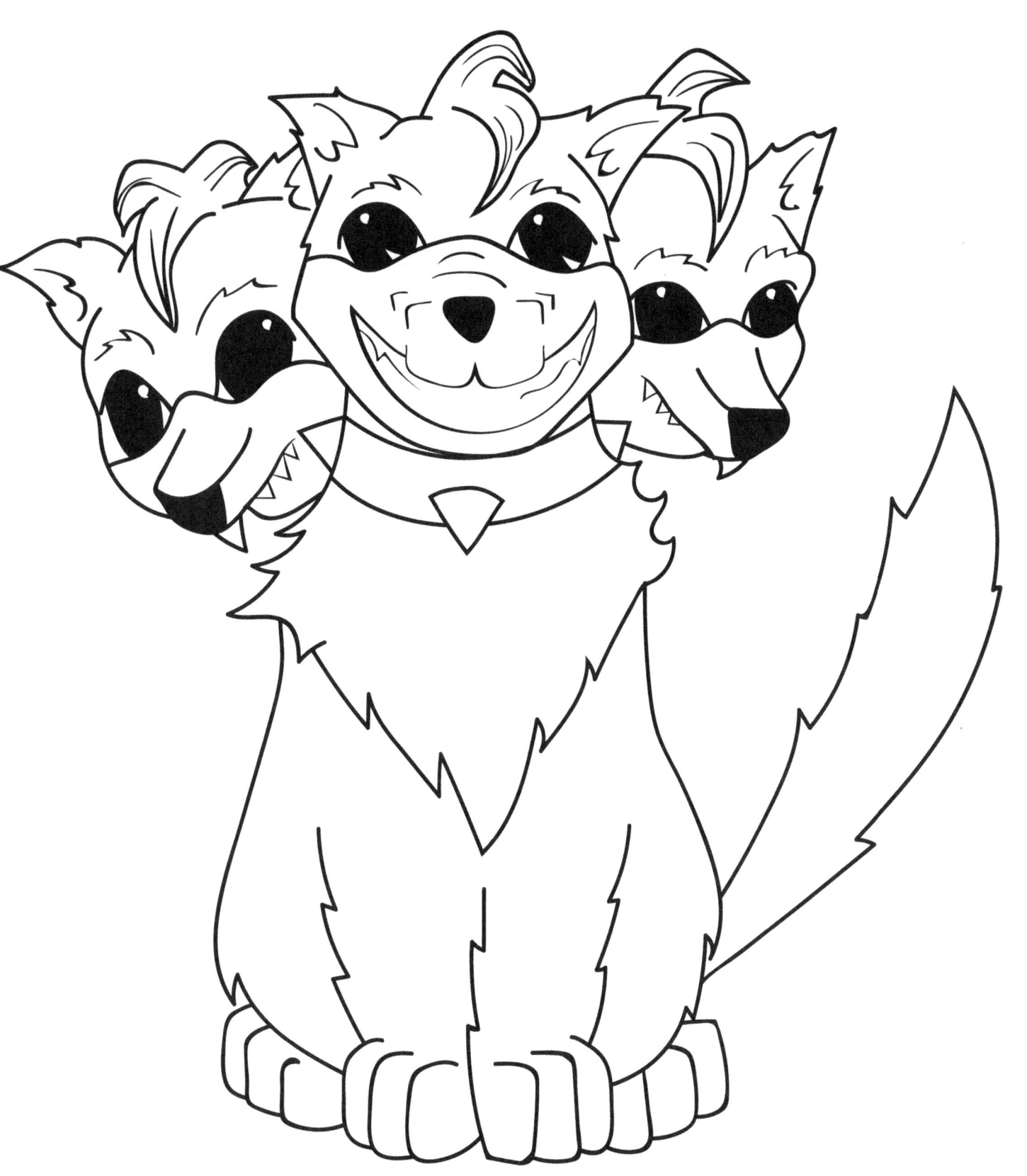

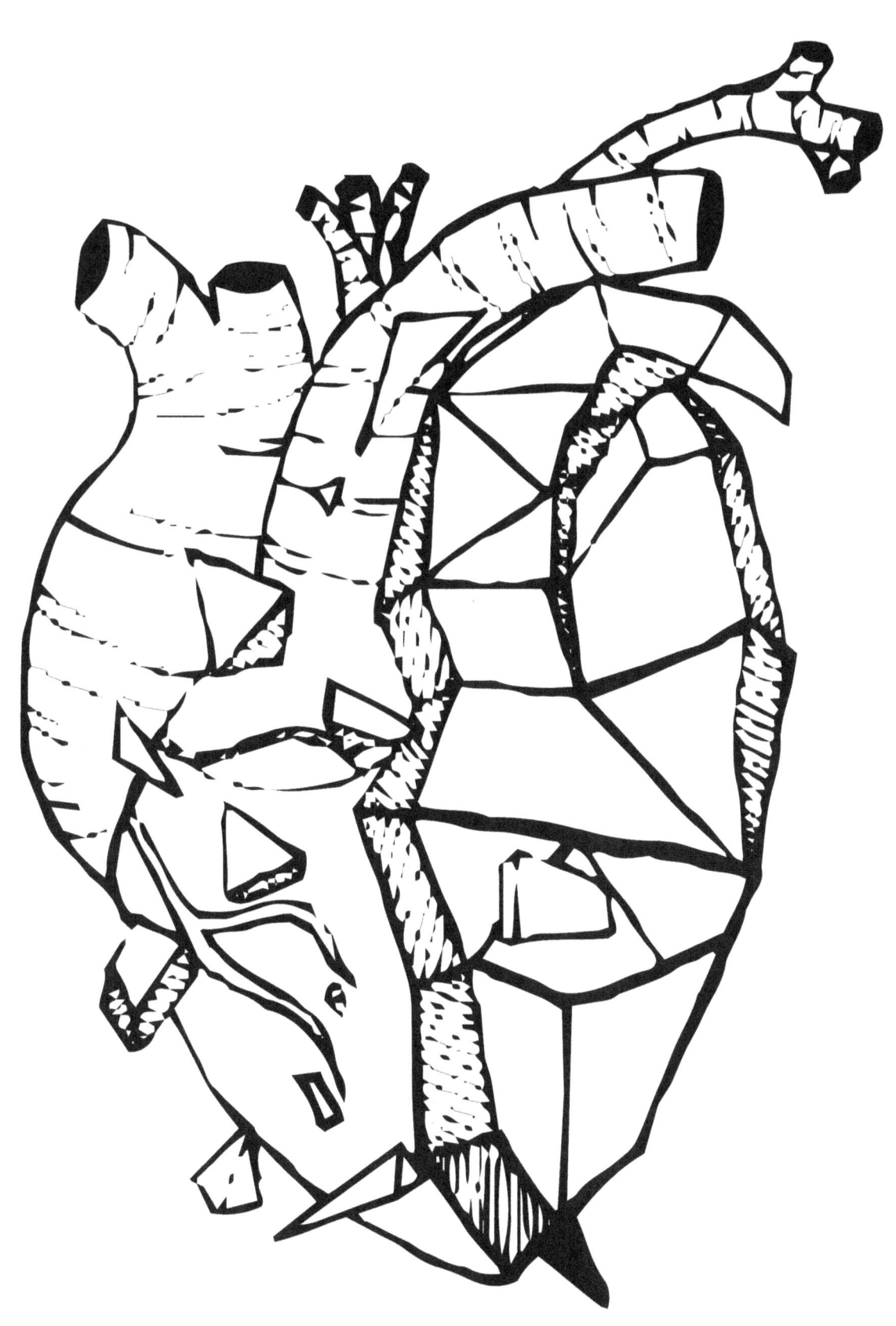

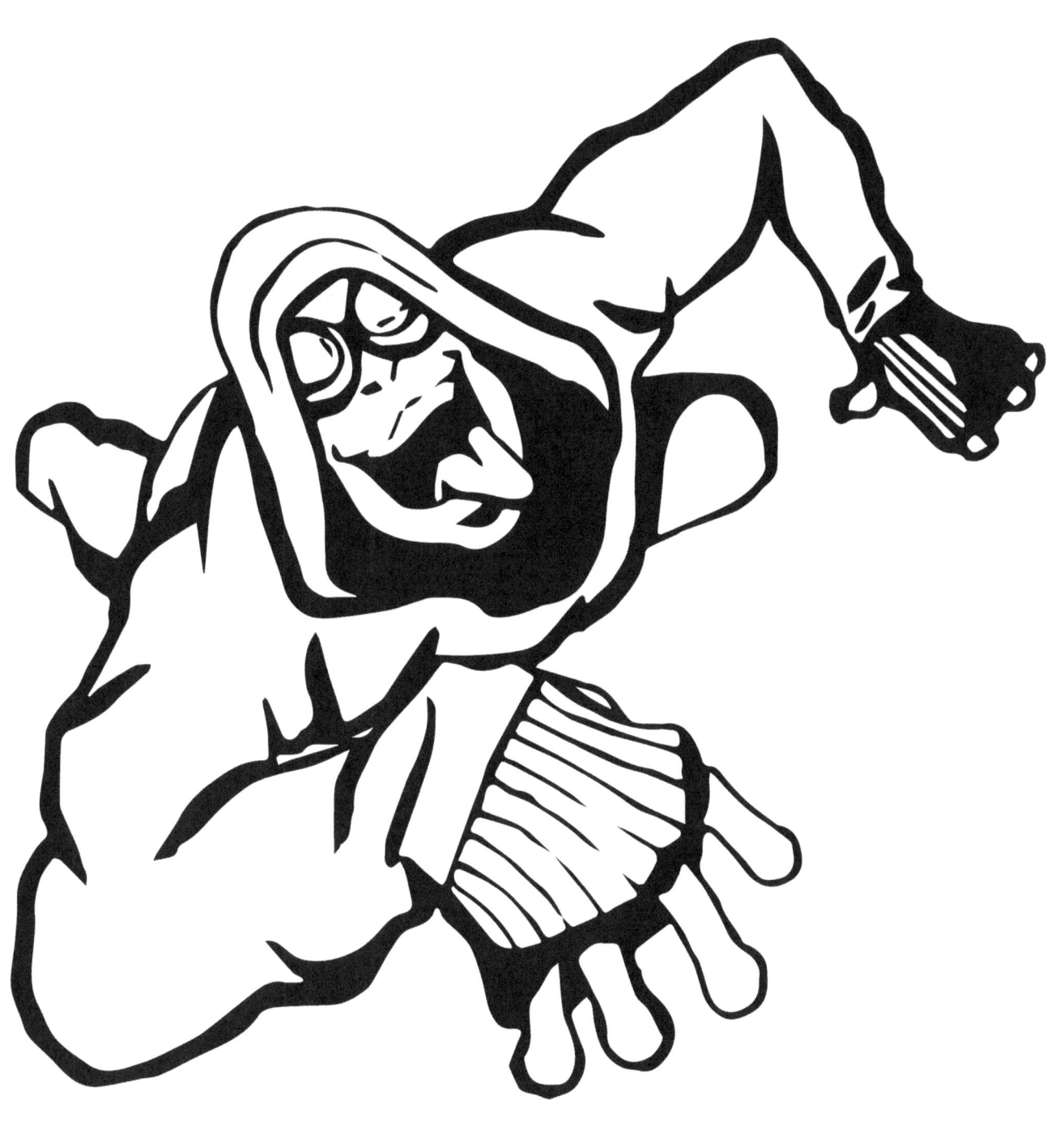

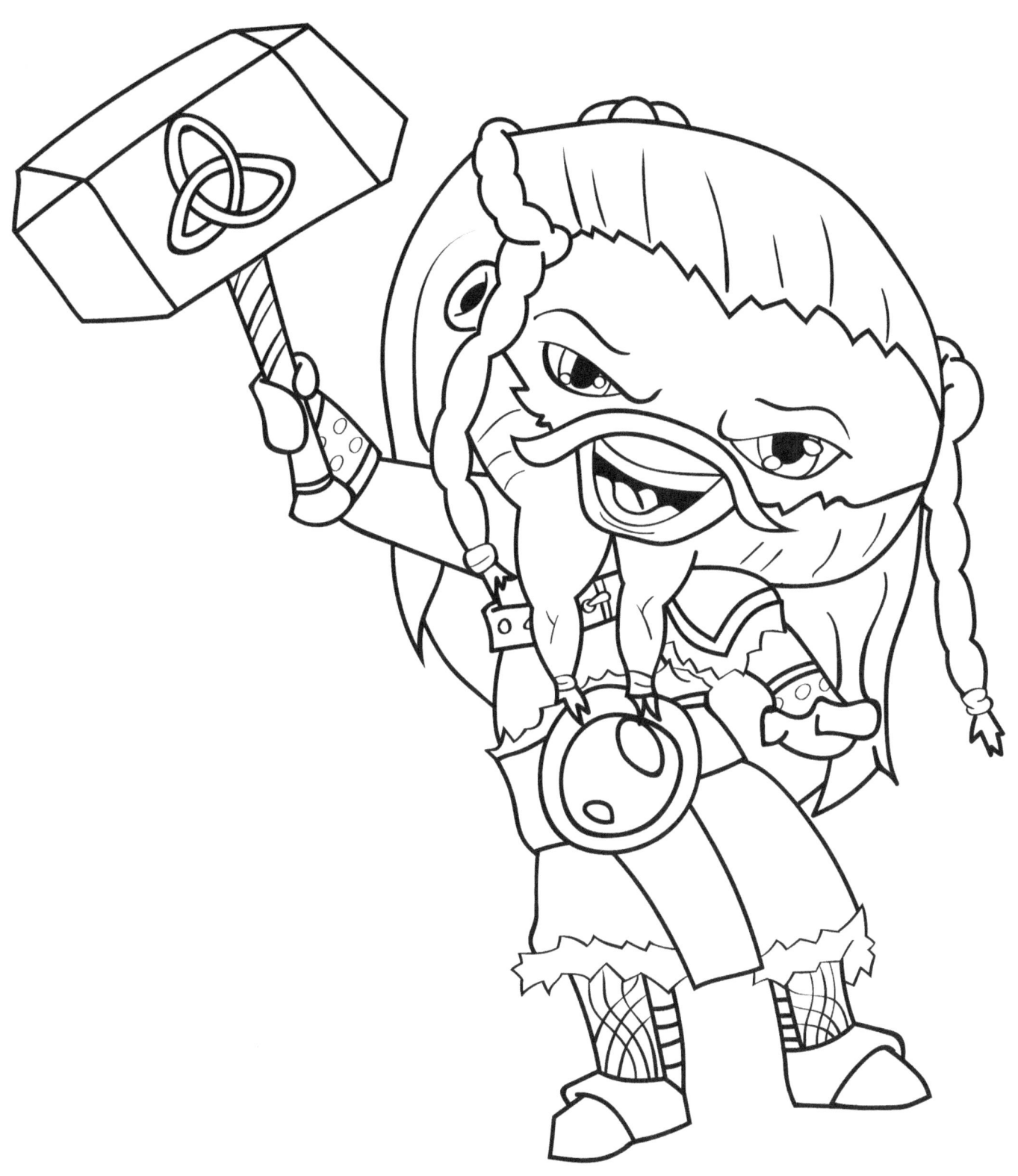

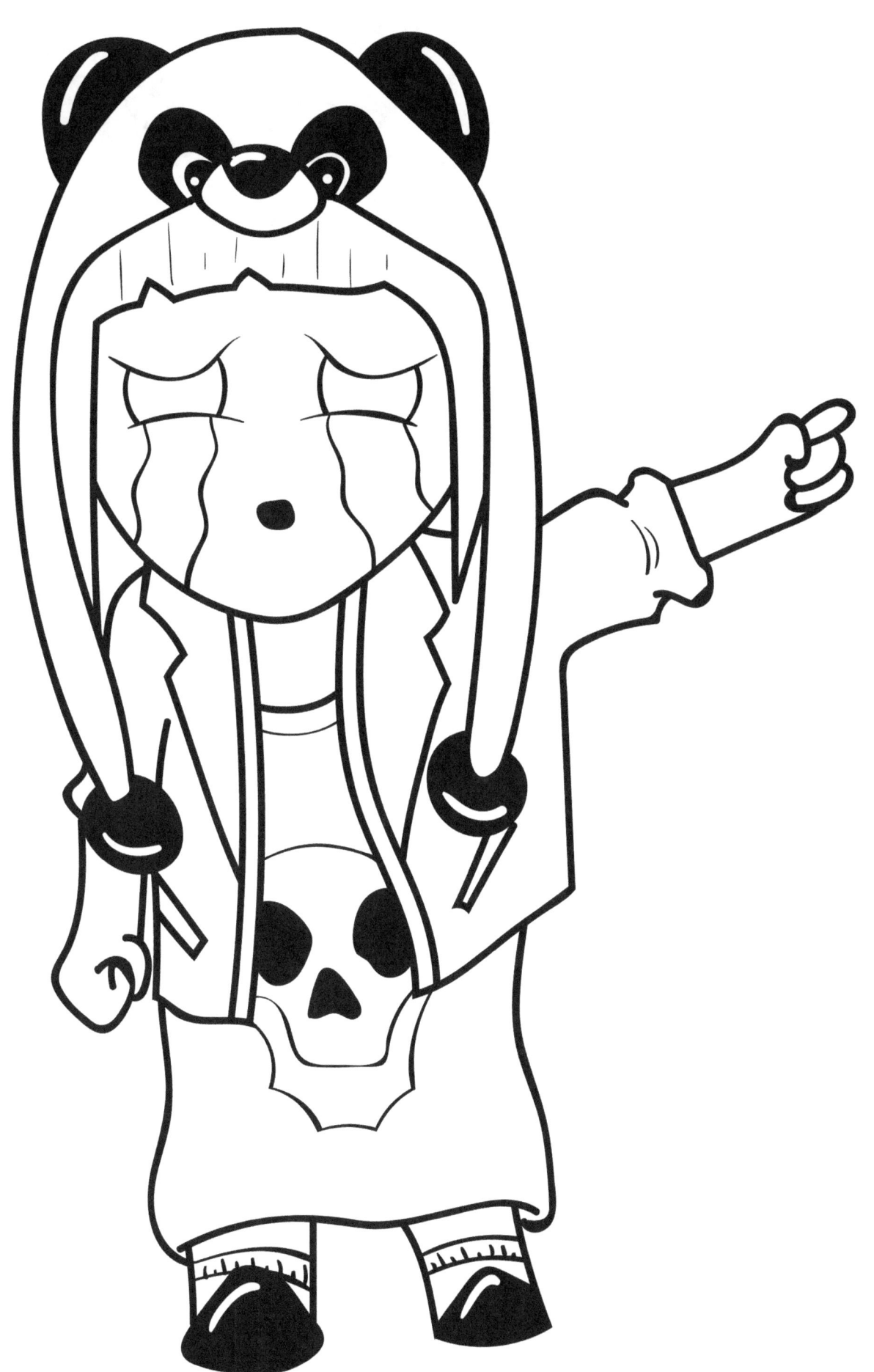

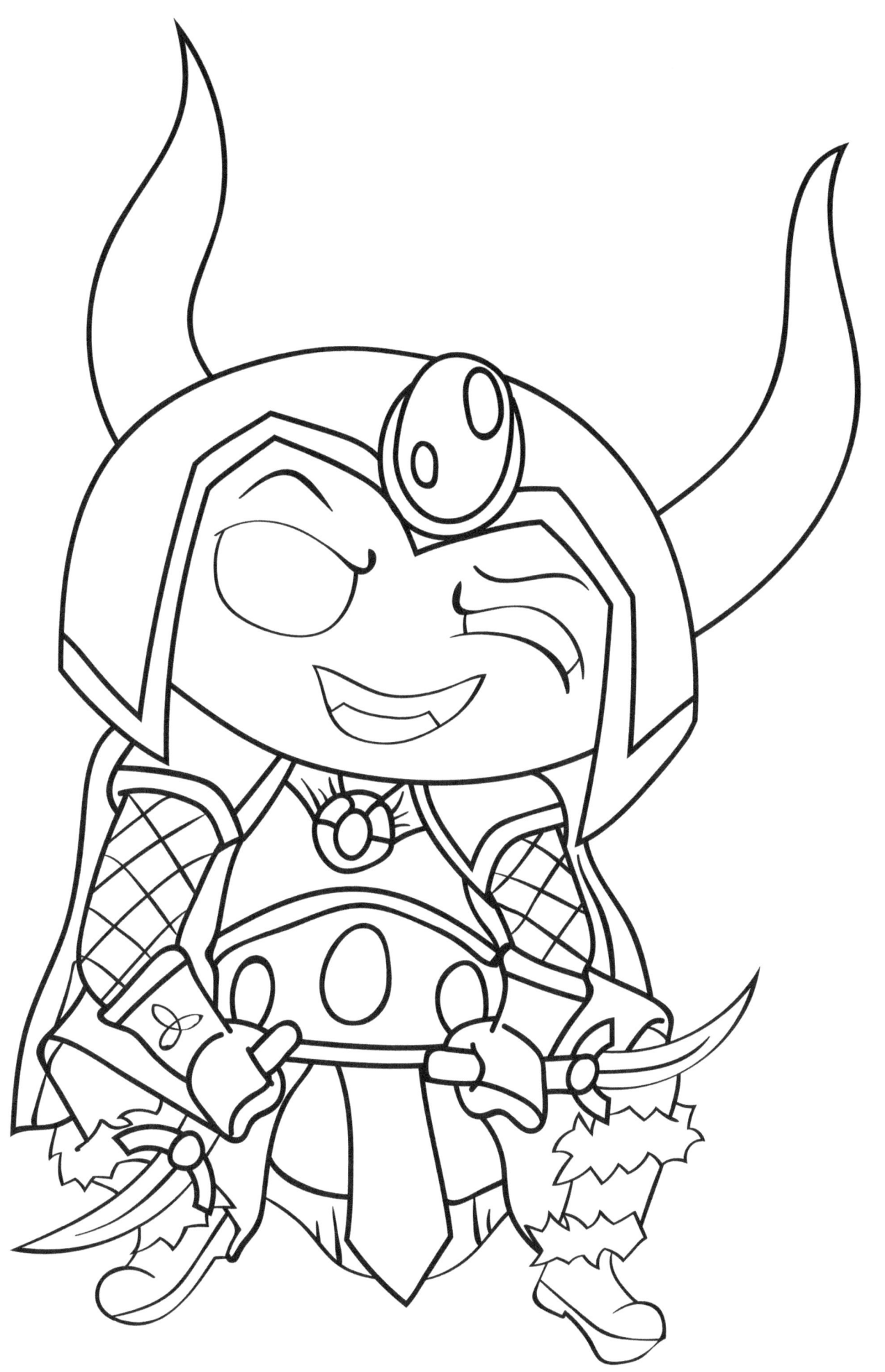

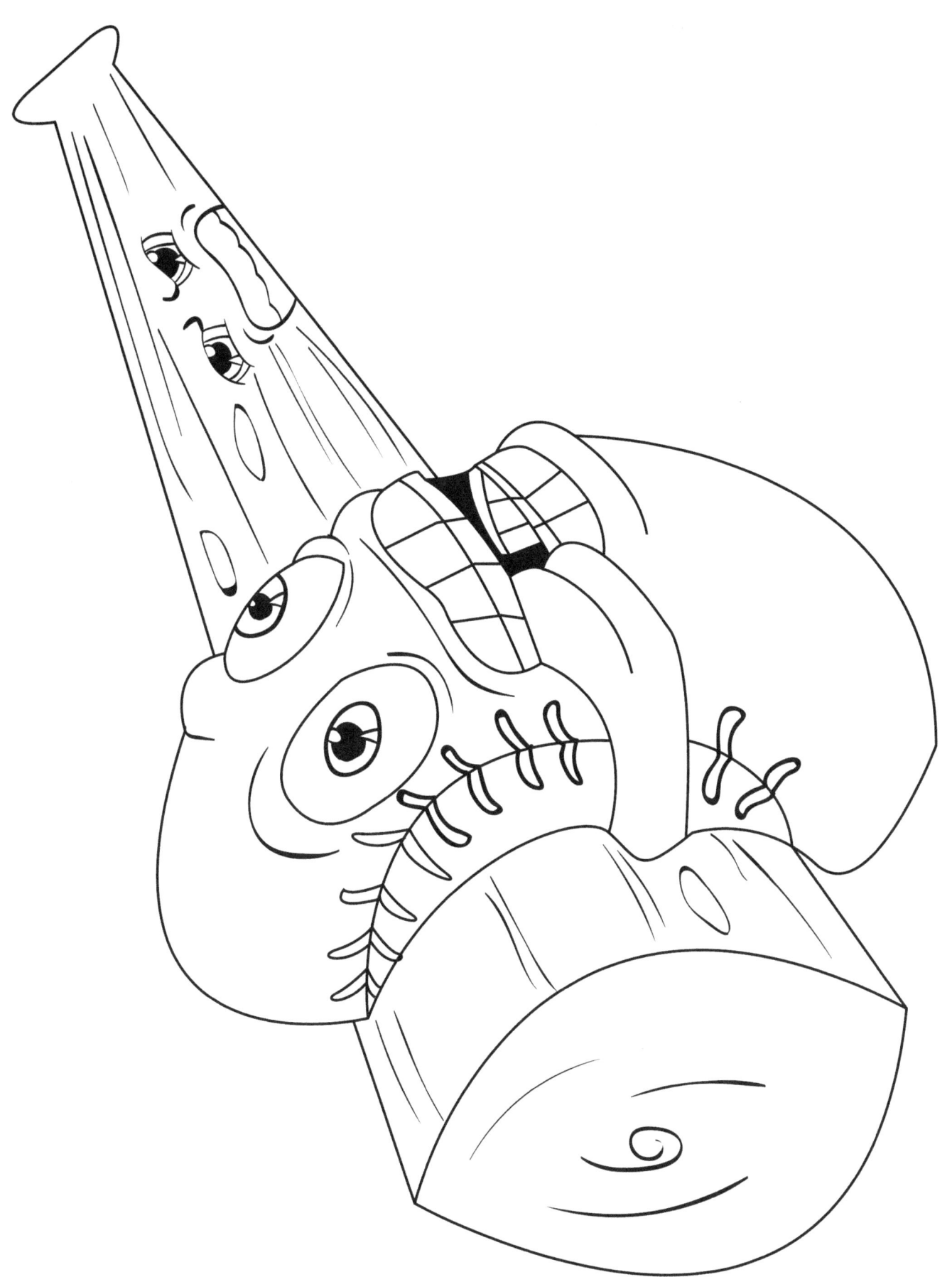

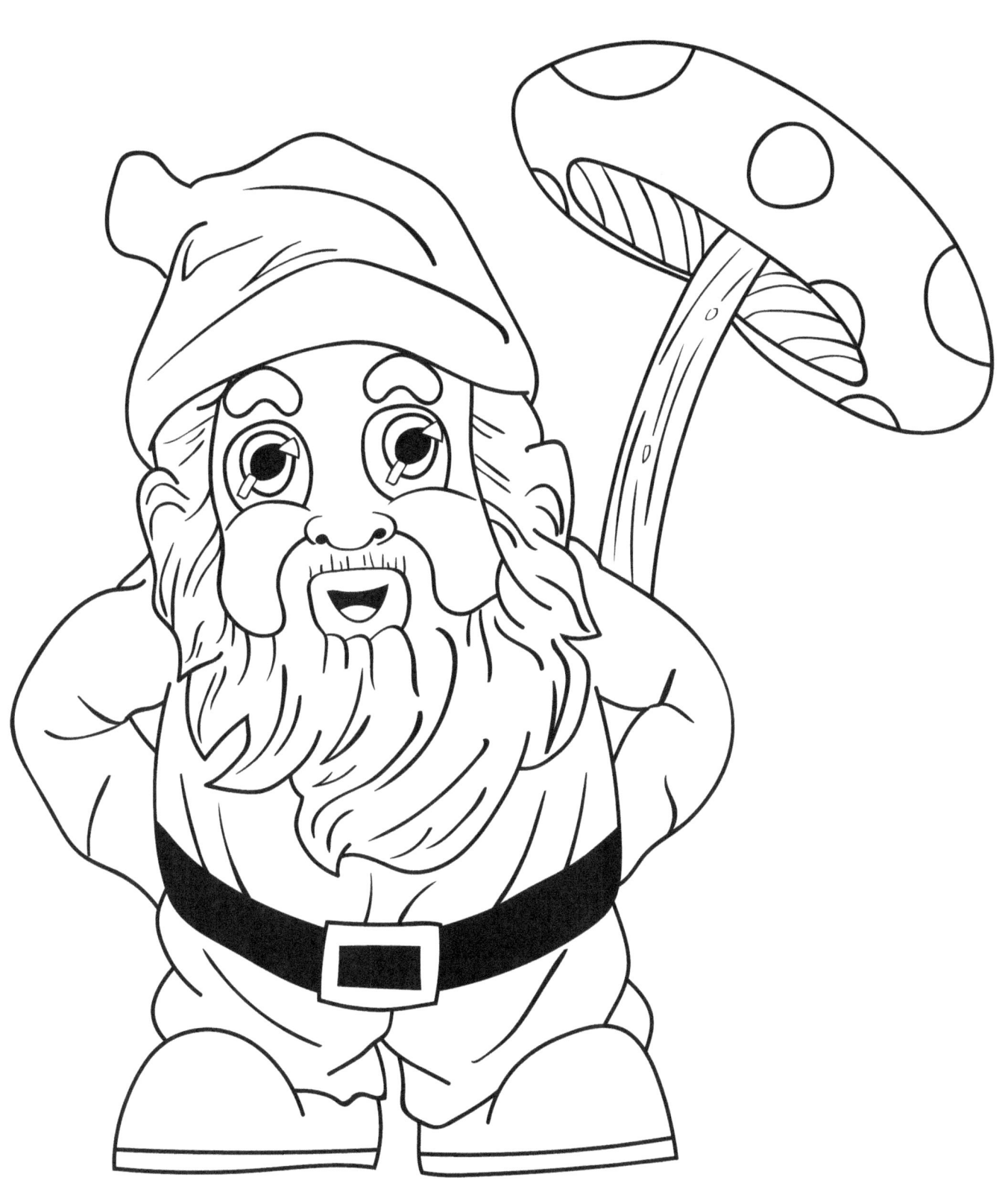

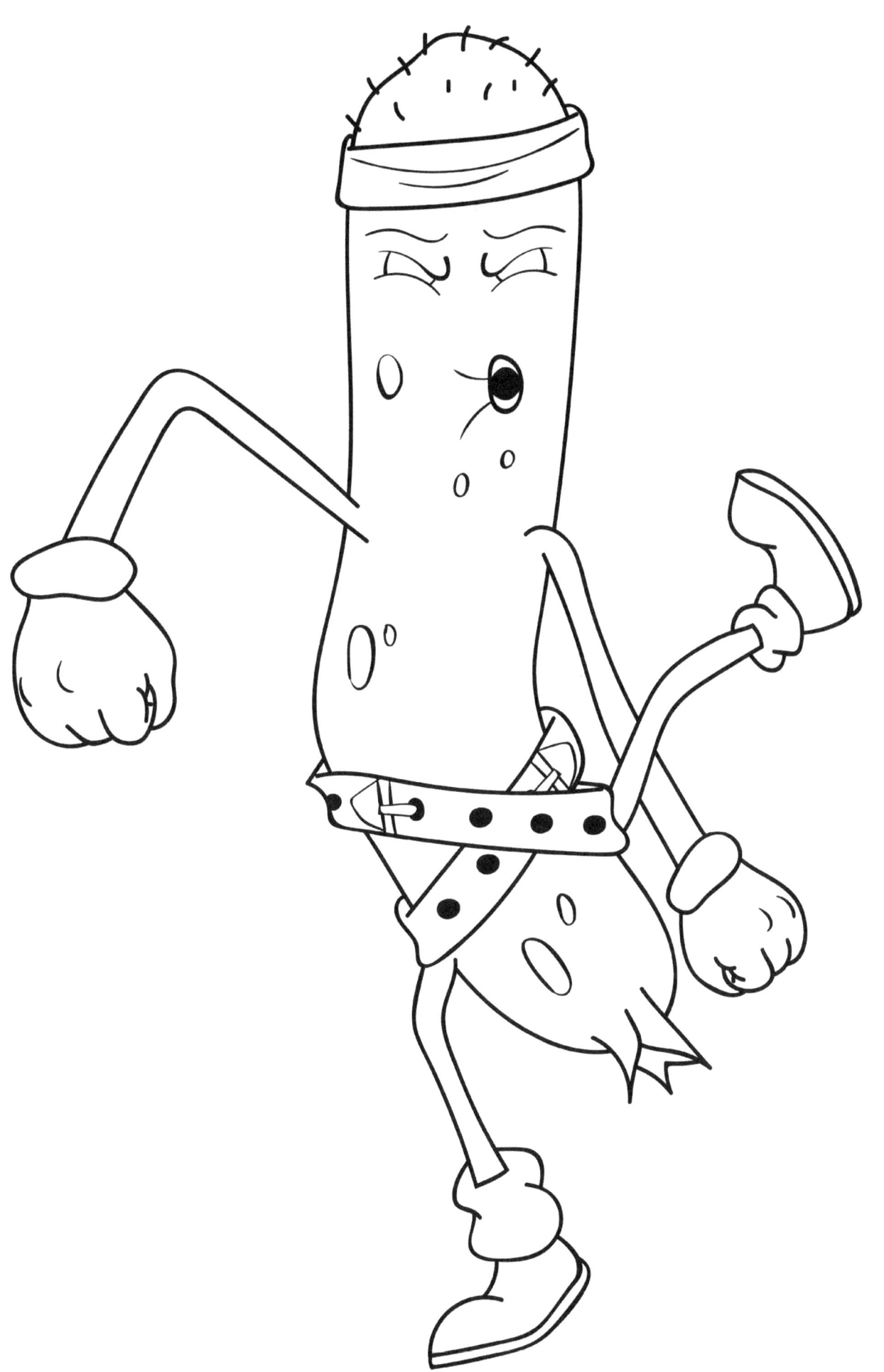

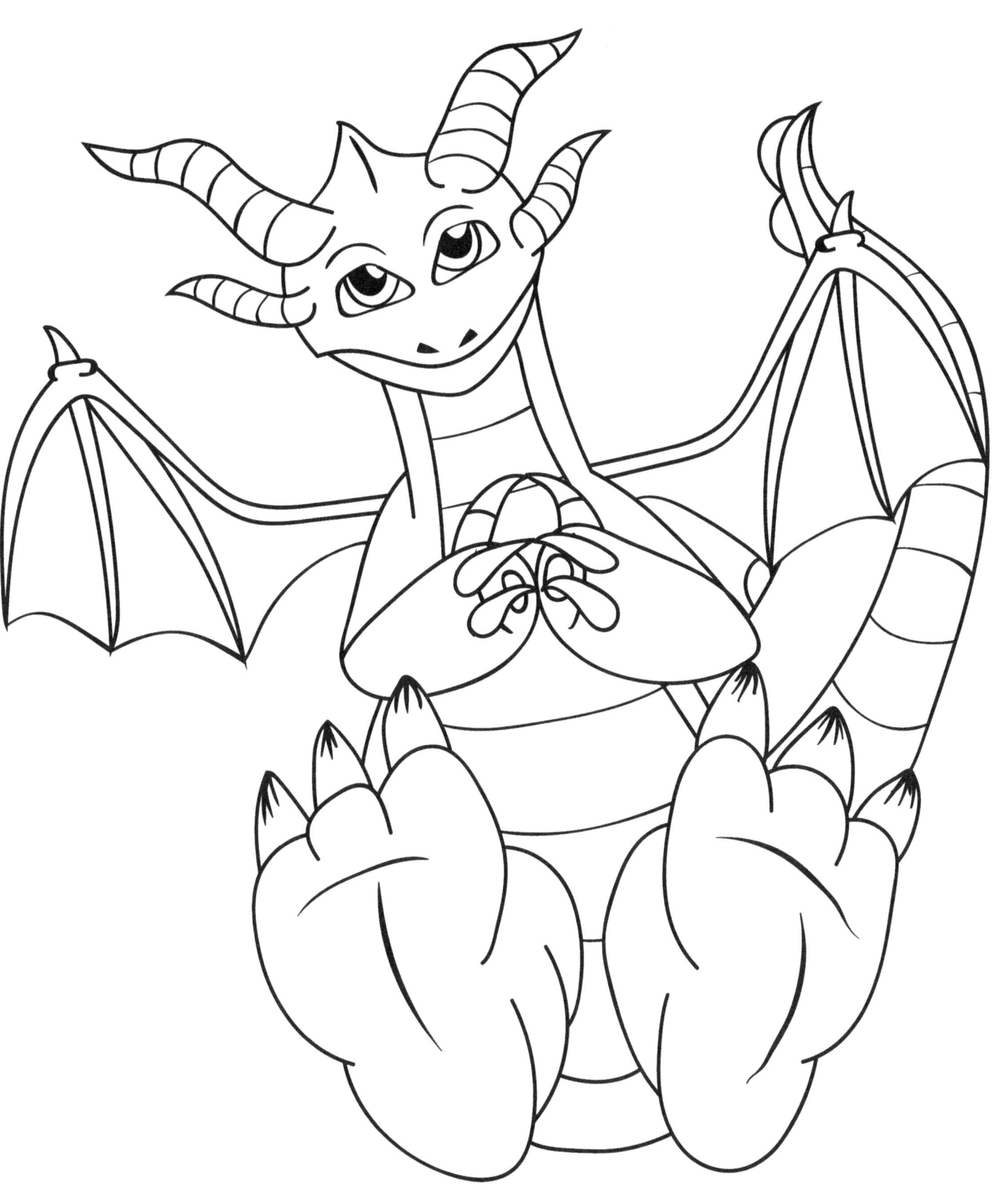

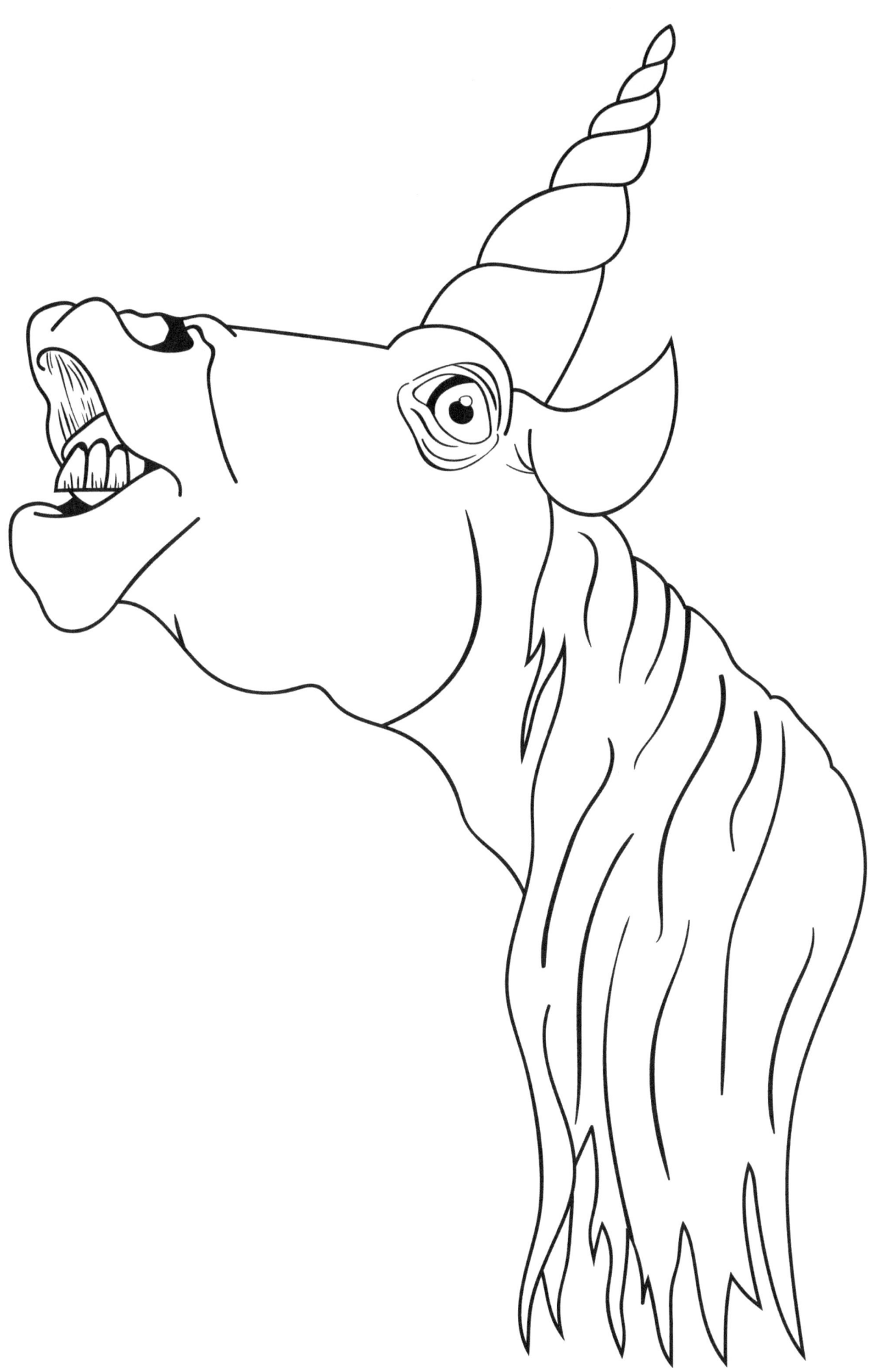

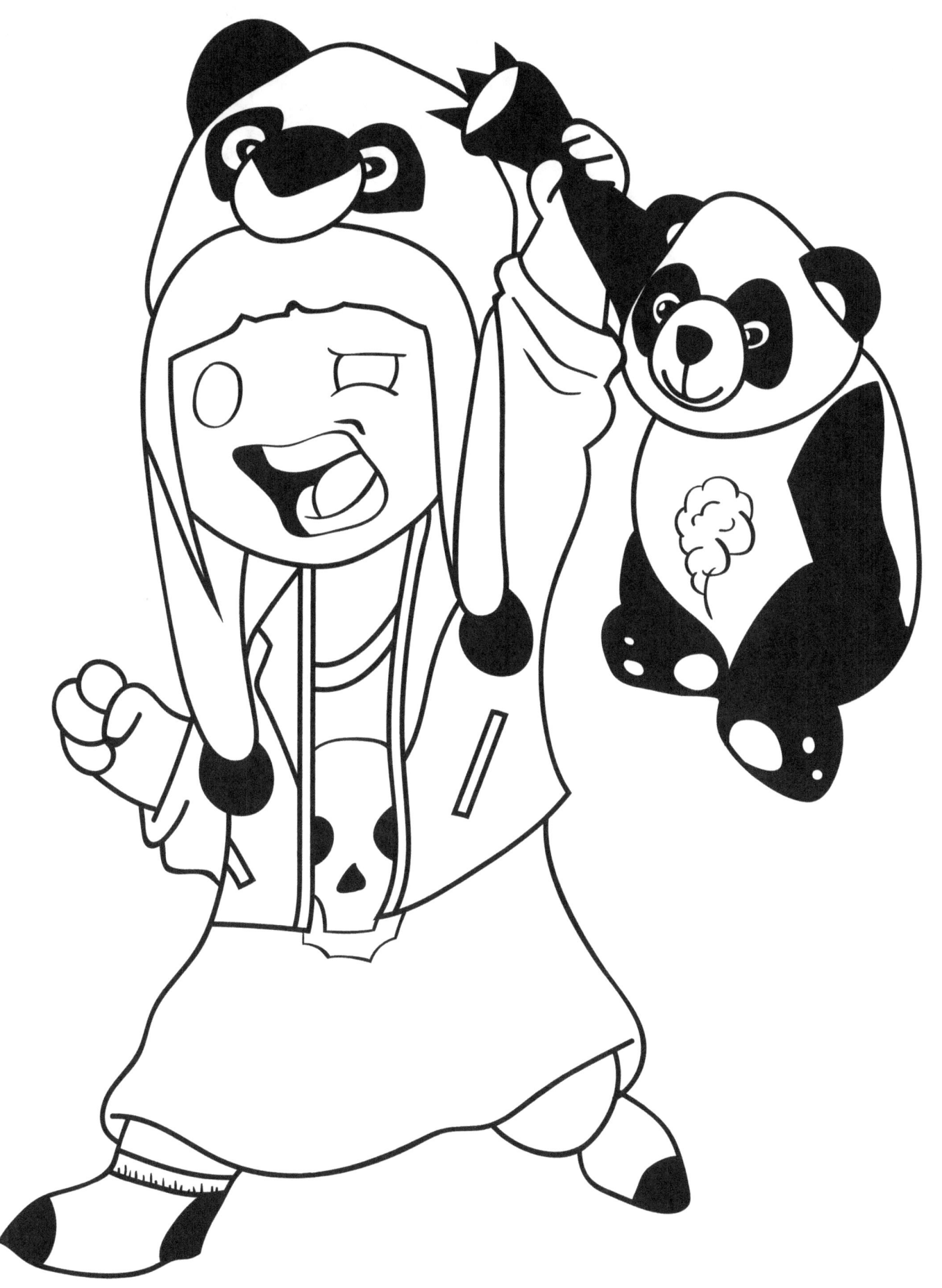

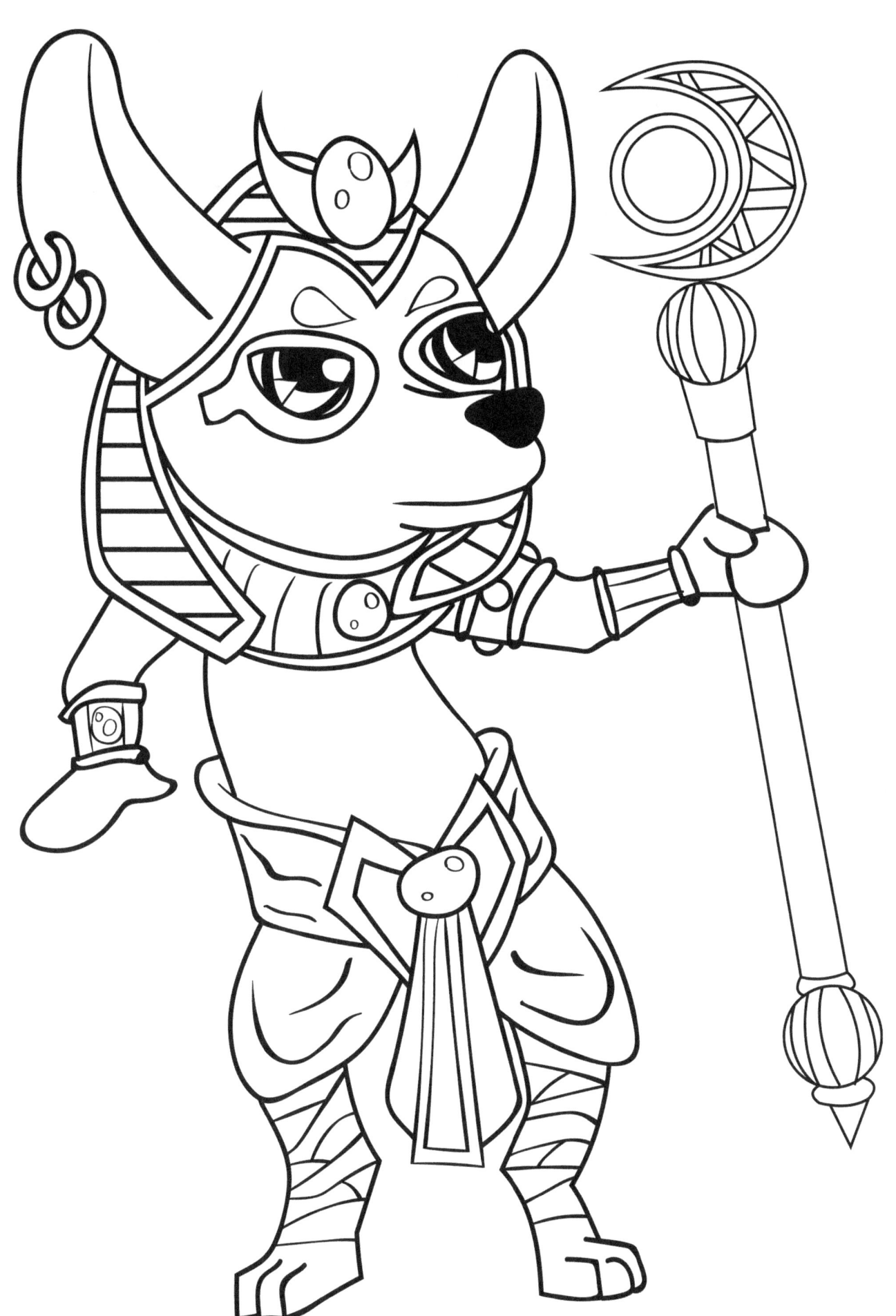

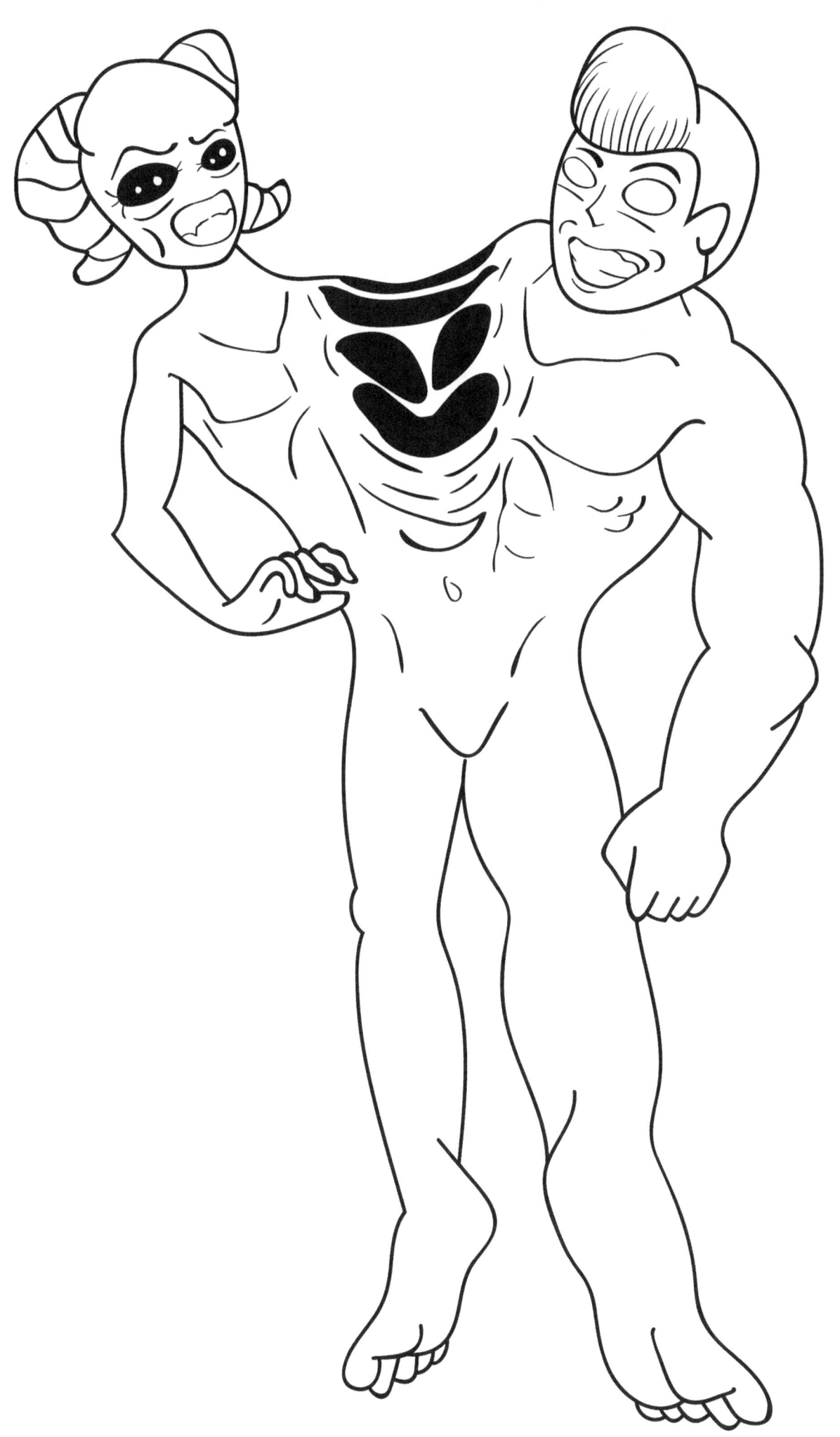

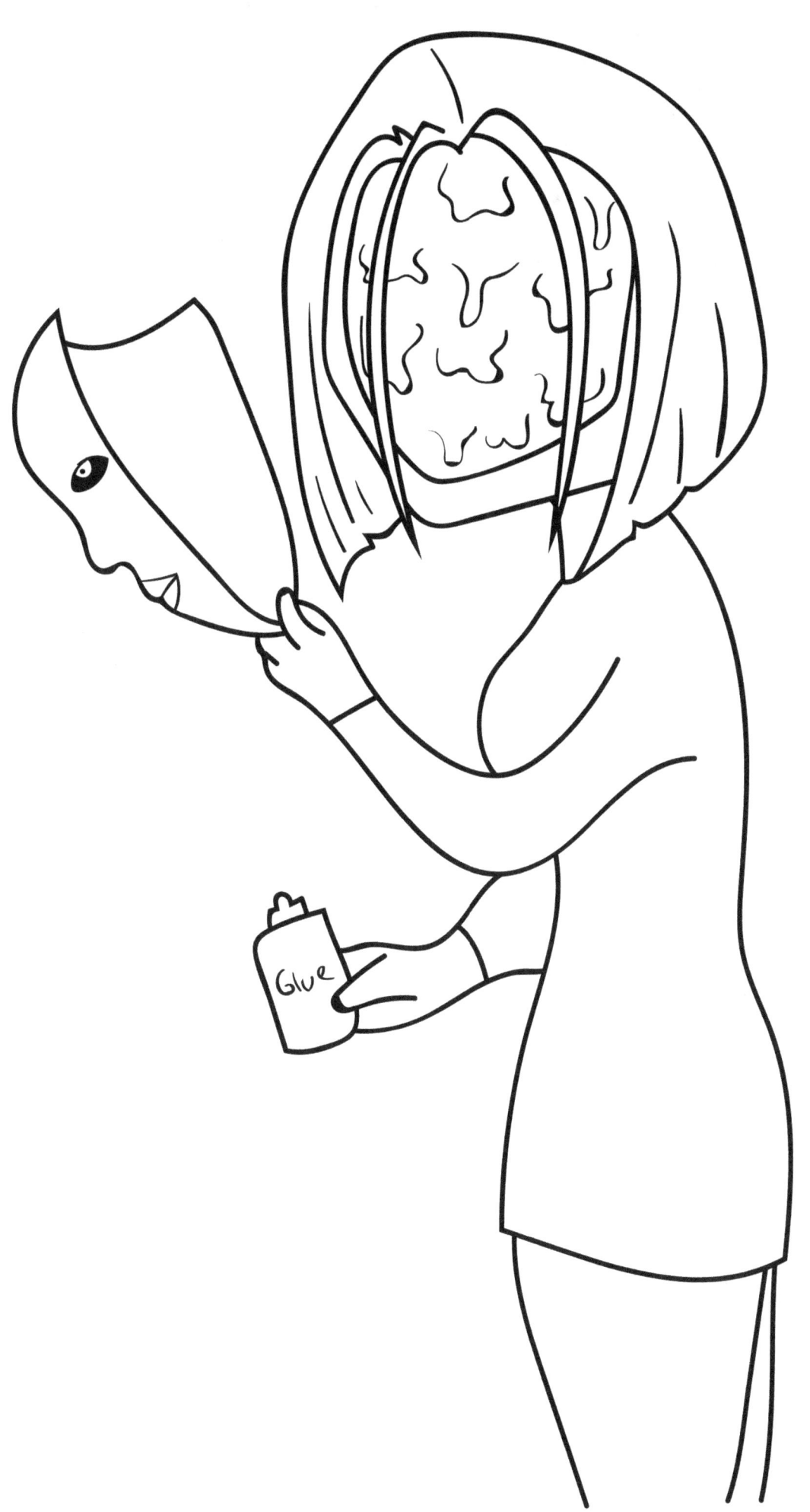

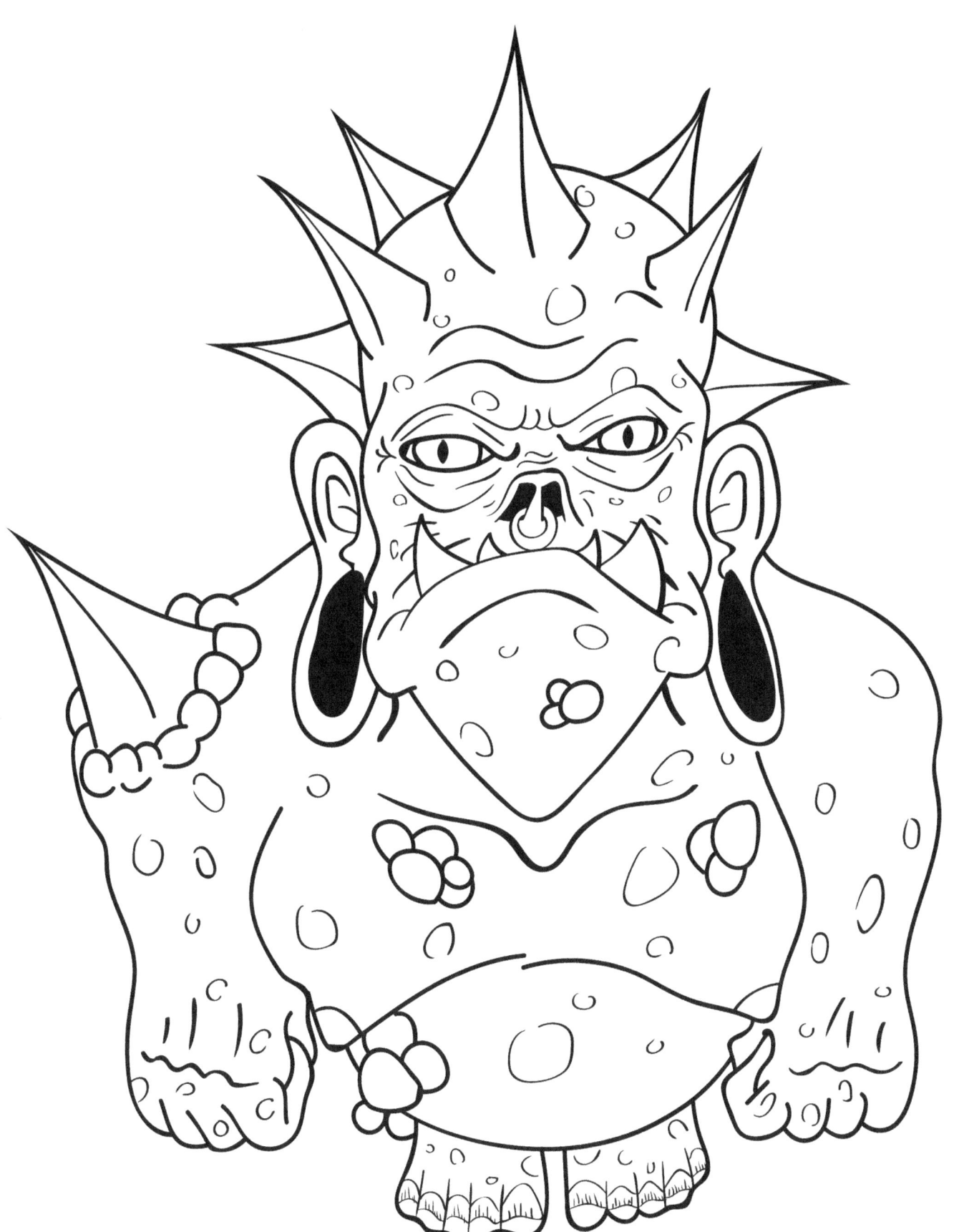

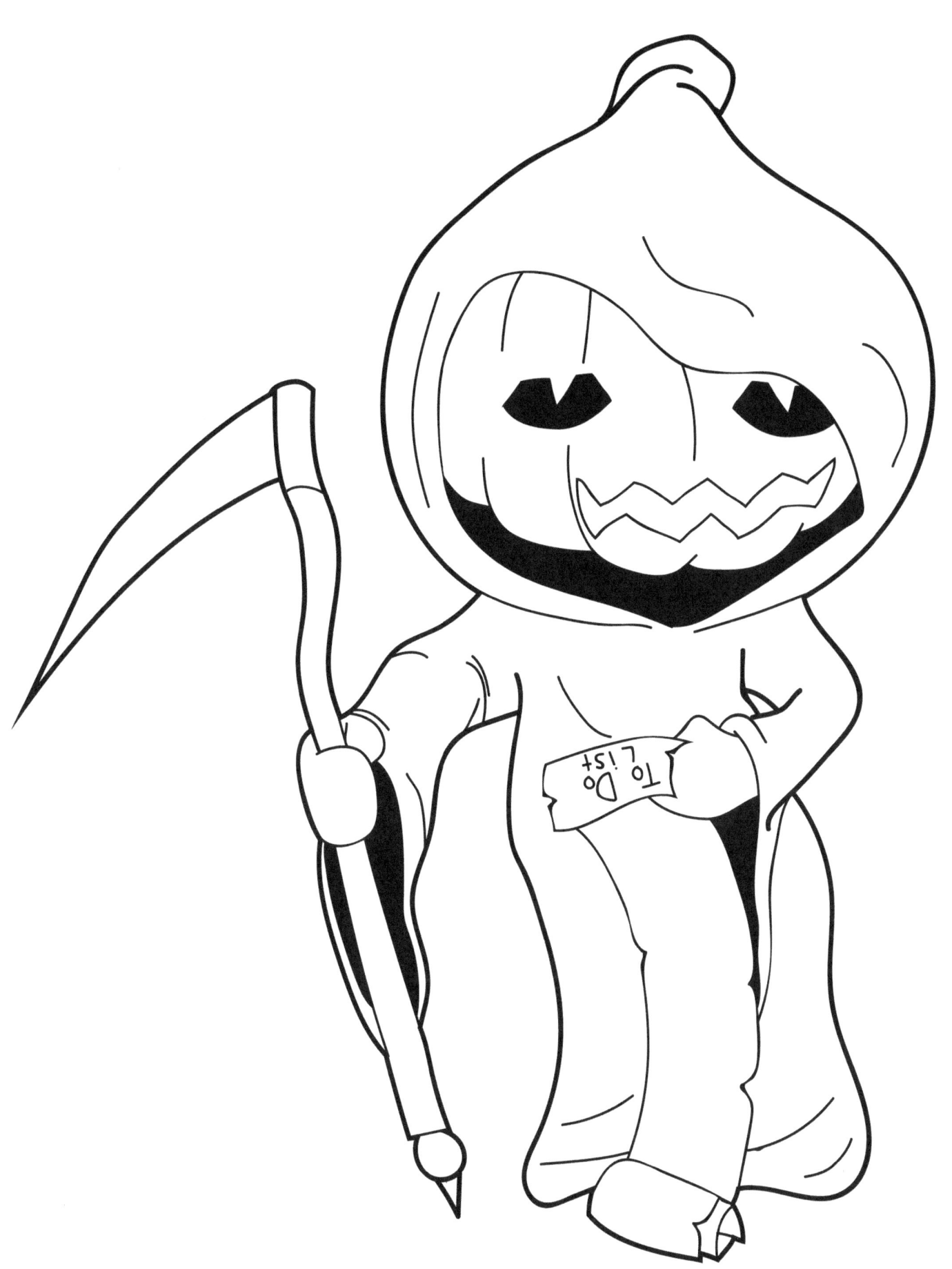

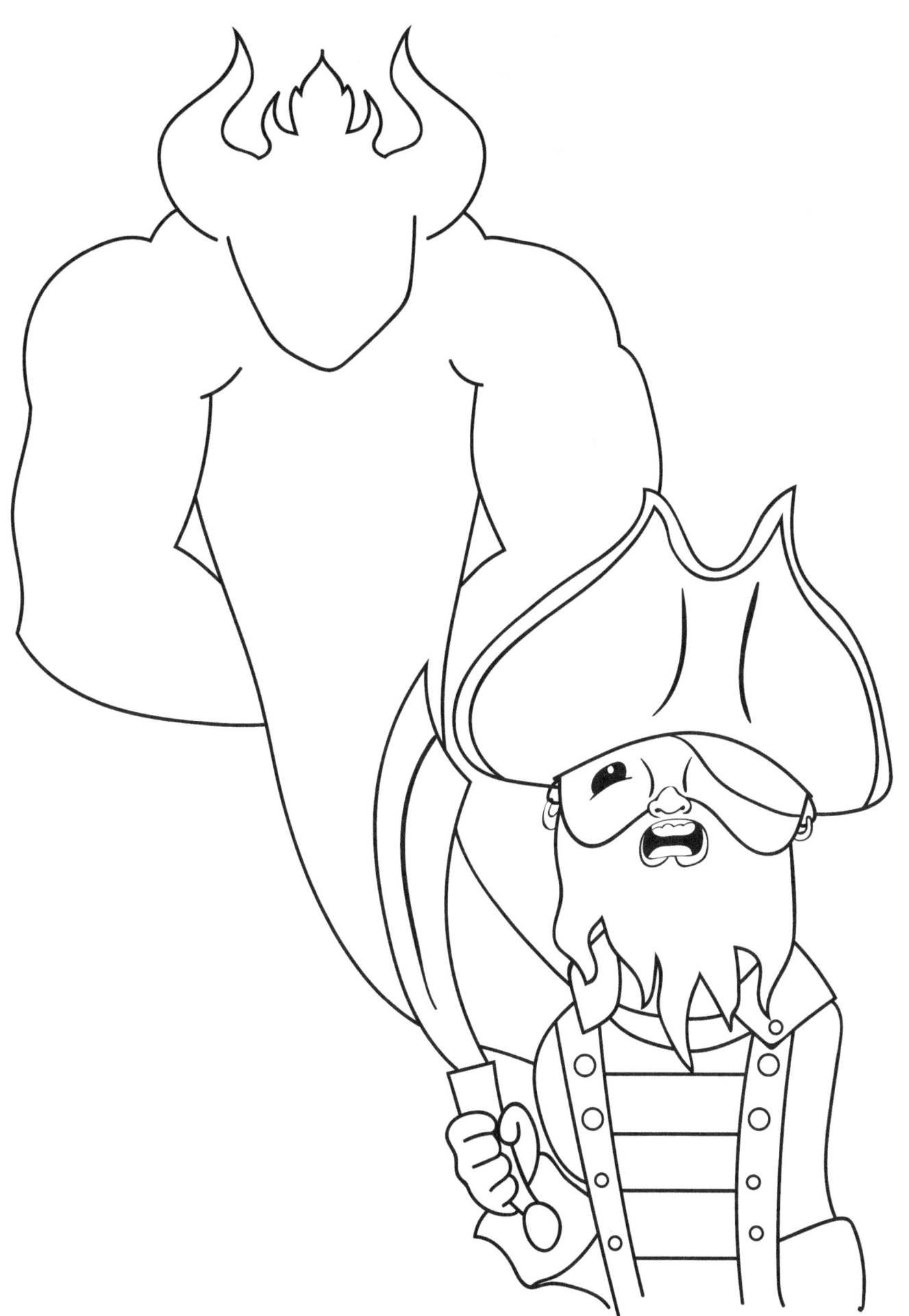

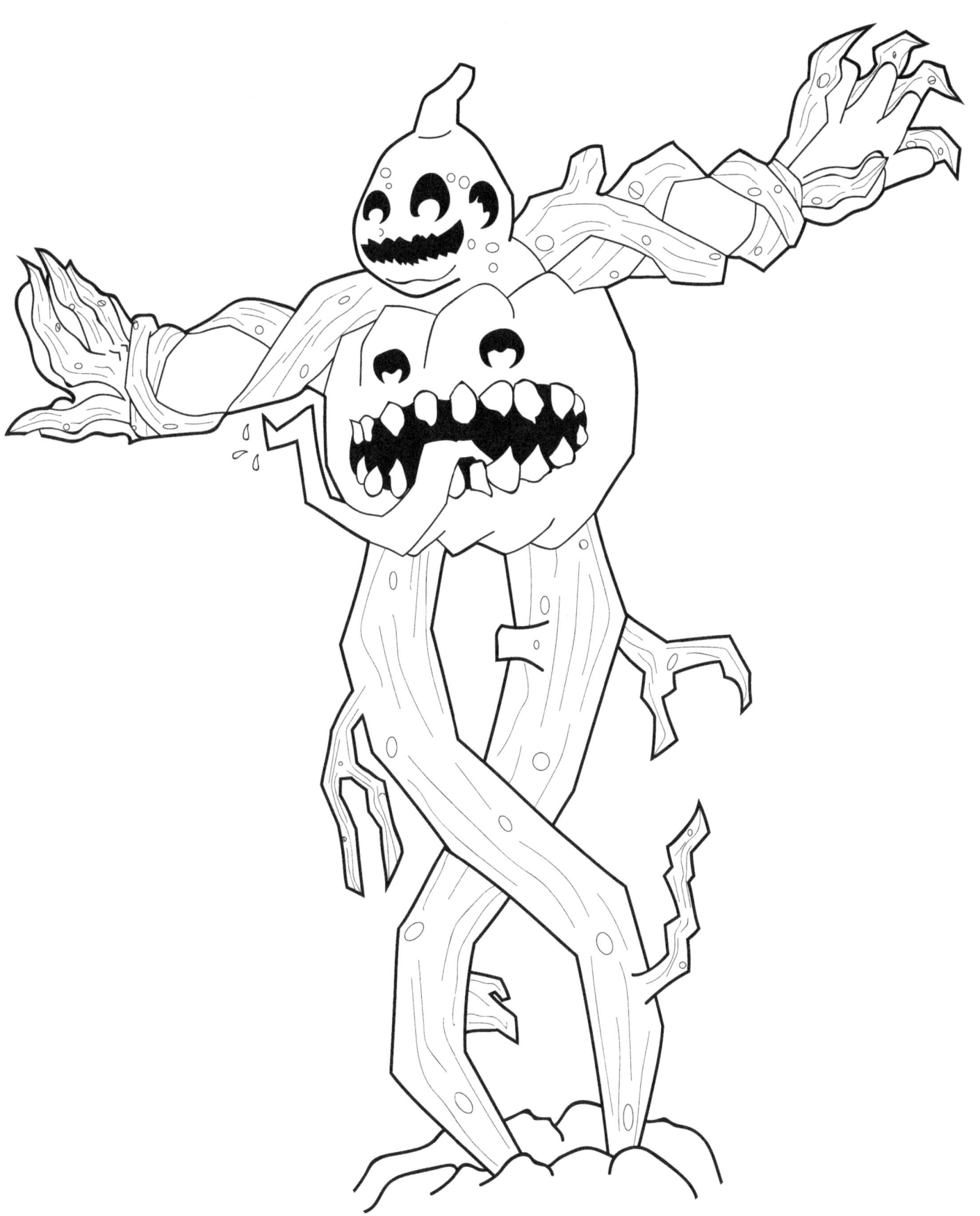

www.ingramcontent.com/pod-product-compliance
Lightning Source LLC
Chambersburg PA
CBHW081613220526
45468CB00010B/2861